ISBN 978-0-332-31303-0
PIBN 11218038

This book is a reproduction of an important historical work. Forgotten Books uses
state-of-the-art technology to digitally reconstruct the work, preserving the original format
whilst repairing imperfections present in the aged copy. In rare cases, an imperfection in
the original, such as a blemish or missing page, may be replicated in our edition. We do,
however, repair the vast majority of imperfections successfully; any imperfections that
remain are intentionally left to preserve the state of such historical works.

English
Français
Deutsche
Italiano
Español
Português

www.forgottenbooks.com

Mythology Photography **Fiction**
Fishing Christianity **Art** Cooking
Essays Buddhism Freemasonry
Medicine **Biology** Music **Ancient
Egypt** Evolution Carpentry Physics
Dance Geology **Mathematics** Fitness
Shakespeare **Folklore** Yoga Marketing
Confidence Immortality Biographies
Poetry **Psychology** Witchcraft
Electronics Chemistry History **Law**
Accounting **Philosophy** Anthropology
Alchemy Drama Quantum Mechanics
Atheism Sexual Health **Ancient History**
Entrepreneurship Languages Sport
Paleontology Needlework Islam
Metaphysics Investment Archaeology
Parenting Statistics Criminology
Motivational

STATE PAPERS,

ETC., ETC., ETC.,

OF

CHESTER A. ARTHUR,

PRESIDENT OF THE UNITED STATES.

WASHINGTON.

1885.

LETTER

ACCEPTING

THE REPUBLICAN NOMINATION FOR VICE-PRESIDENT.

JULY 15, 1880.

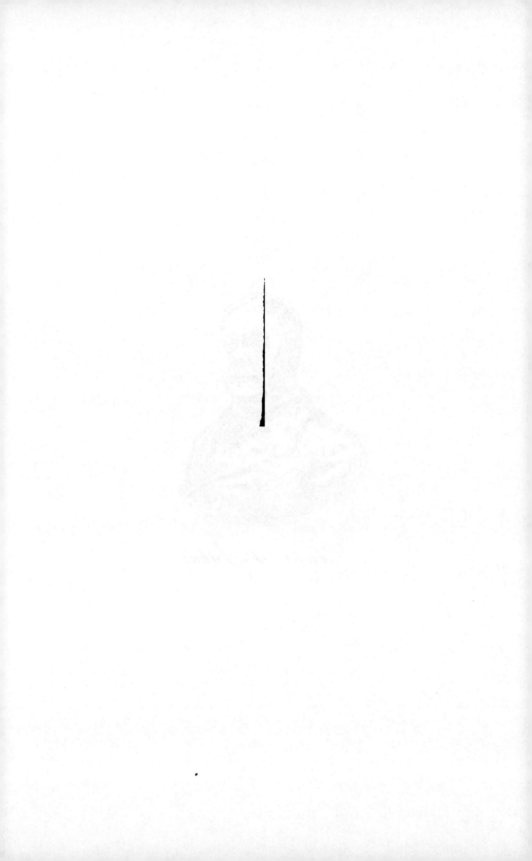

Chester A. Arthur.

INAUGURAL ADDRESS

AS

PRESIDENT OF THE UNITED STATES,

SEPTEMBER 22, 1881.

INAUGURAL ADDRESS.

For the fourth time in the history of the Republic its Chief Magistrate has been removed by death. All hearts are filled with grief and horror at the hideous crime which has darkened our land; and the memory of the murdered President, his protracted sufferings, his unyielding fortitude, the example and achievements of his life, and the pathos of his death will forever illumine the pages of our history.

For the fourth time the officer elected by the people and ordained by the Constitution to fill a vacancy so created is called to assume the Executive Chair. The wisdom of our fathers, foreseeing even the most dire possibilities, made sure that the Government should never be imperilled because of the uncertainty of human life. Men may die but the fabrics of our free institutions remain unshaken. No higher or more assuring proof could exist of the strength and permanance of popular government than the fact that, though the chosen of the people be struck down, his constitutional successor is peacefully installed, without shock or strain, except the sorrow which mourns the bereavement. All the noble aspirations of my lamented predecessor which found expression in his life, the measures devised and suggested during his brief administration to correct abuses, to enforce economy, to advance prosperity, and to promote the general welfare, to insure domestic security and maintain friendly and honorable relations with the nations of the earth, will be garnered in the hearts of the people, and it will be my earnest endeavor to profit and to see that the nation shall profit by his example and experience.

Prosperity blesses our country, our fiscal policy is fixed by law, is well grounded and generally approved. No threatening issue mars our foreign intercourse, and the wisdom, integrity, and thrift of our people may be trusted to continue undisturbed the present assured career of peace, tranquillity, and welfare. The gloom and anxiety which have enshrouded the country must make repose especially welcome now. No demand for speedy legislation has been heard; no adequate occasion is apparent for an unusual session of Congress. The Constitution defines the functions and powers of the Executive as clearly as those of either of the other two departments of the Government, and he must answer for the just exercise of the discretion it permits and the performance of the duties it imposes. Summoned to these high duties and responsibilities, and profoundly conscious of their magnitude and gravity, I assume the trust imposed by the Constitution, relying for aid on Divine guidance and the virtue, patriotism, and intelligence of the American people.

PROCLAMATION

CONCERNING

THE DEATH OF PRESIDENT GARFIELD,

SEPTEMBER 22, 1881.

13

PROCLAMATION.

A PROCLAMATION.

Whereas, in His inscrutable wisdom, it has pleased God to remove from us the illustrious head of the Nation, James A. Garfield, late President of the United States; and

Whereas, it is fitting that the deep grief which fills all hearts should manifest itself with one accord toward the throne of Infinite Grace, and that we should bow before the Almighty and seek from Him that consolation in our affliction and that sanctification of our loss which He is able and willing to vouchsafe;

Now, therefore, in obedience to sacred duty and in accordance with the desire of the people, I, CHESTER A. ARTHUR, President of the United States of America, do hereby appoint Monday, next, the twenty-sixth day of September—on which day the remains of our honored and beloved dead will be consigned to their last resting-place on earth—to be observed throughout the United States as a day of humiliation and mourning; and I earnestly recommend all the people to assemble on that day in their respective places of divine worship, there to render alike their tribute of sorrowful submission to the will of Almighty God and of reverence and love for the memory and character of our late Chief Magistrate.

In witness whereof I have hereunto set my hand and caused the seal of the United States to be affixed.

Done at the city of Washington the twenty-second day of September, in the year of our Lord eighteen hundred and eighty-one, and of the Independence of the United States of America the one hundred and sixth.

[SEAL.]   CHESTER A. ARTHUR.

By the President:

    JAMES G. BLAINE,
        Secretary of State.

PROCLAMATION

SPECIAL SESSION OF THE SENATE OCTOBER 10, 1881,

SEPTEMBER 23, 1881.

————————

PROCLAMATION.

BY THE PRESIDENT OF THE UNITED STATES OF AMERICA.

A PROCLAMATION.

Whereas objects of interest to the United States require that the Senate should be convened at an early day to receive and act upon such communications as may be made to it on the part of the Executive:

Now, therefore, I, CHESTER A. ARTHUR, President of the United States, have considered it to be my duty to issue this, my proclamation, declaring that an extraordinary occasion requires the Senate of the United States to convene for the transaction of business at the Capitol, in the city of Washington, on Monday, the tenth day of October next, at twelve o'clock noon on that day, of which all who shall at that time be entitled to act as members of that body are hereby required to take notice.

Given under my hand and the seal of the United States, at Washington, the twenty-third day of September, in the year of our Lord one thousand eight hundred and eighty-one, and of the Independence of the United States the one hundred and sixth.

[SEAL.]   CHESTER A. ARTHUR.

By the President:

    JAMES G. BLAINE,
        Secretary of State.

19

ADDRESS

AT THE

YORKTOWN CENTENNIAL CELEBRATION,

OCTOBER 19, 1881.

21

ADDRESS.

Upon this soil, one hundred years ago, our forefathers brought to a successful issue their heroic struggle for independence. Here and then was established, and as we trust made forever secure upon this continent that principle of government which is the very foundation of our political system—the sovereignty of the people.

The resentments that attended and for a time survived the clash of arms have long since ceased to animate our breasts. It is with no feeling of exultation over a defeated foe that we summon up to-day remembrance of the events that have made holy the ground whereon we tread. Surely no such unworthy sentiment could find harbor in our hearts, profoundly thrilled as they are by the expressions of sorrow and sympathy which our national bereavement has lately evoked from the people of England and from their august sovereign.

It is well that we have gathered here to refresh our souls with the contemplation of the unfaltering patriotism, the sturdy zeal, the sublime faith which achieved the results we now commemorate; for so, if we learn aright the lesson of the hour, shall we be incited to transmit to the generations that shall follow, the precious legacy which our fathers transmitted to us—the love of liberty protected by law.

Of the historic scene that was here enacted no feature was more prominent, and none more inspiring than the participation of our gallant allies from across the sea. It was their presence that gave fresh and vigorous impulse to the hopes of our countrymen when well nigh disheartened by a long series of disasters. It was their noble and generous aid, extended in the darkest period of the struggle, that sped the coming of our triumph and made the capitulation at Yorktown possible a century ago. To their descendants and representatives who are present as the honored guests of the Nation, it

A PROCLAMATION.

It has long been the pious custom of our people, with the closing of the year, to look back upon the blessings brought to them in the changing course of the seasons, and to return solemn thanks to the All-giving Source from Whom they flow. And although at this period, when the falling leaf admonishes us that the time of our sacred duty is at hand, our Nation still lies in the shadow of a great bereavement, and the mourning which has filled our hearts still finds its sorrowful expression toward the God before Whom we but lately bowed in grief and supplication, yet the countless benefits which have showered upon us during the past twelvemonth call for our fervent gratitude, and make it fitting that we should rejoice with thankfulness that the Lord, in His infinite mercy, has most signally favored our country and our people. Peace without and prosperity within have been vouchsafed to us; no pestilence has visited our shores; the abundant privileges of freedom which our fathers left us in their wisdom are still our increasing heritage; and if, in parts of our vast domain, sore affliction has visited our brethren in their forest homes, yet even this calamity has been tempered and in a manner sanctified by the generous compassion for the sufferers which has been called forth throughout our land. For all these things, it is meet that the voice of the Nation should go up to God in devout homage.

Wherefore I, CHESTER A. ARTHUR, President of the United States, do recommend that all the people observe Thursday, the twenty-fourth day of November instant, as a day of National Thanksgiving and Prayer, by ceasing, so far as may be, from their secular labors, and meeting in their several places of worship, there to join in ascribing honor and praise to Almighty God, Whose goodness has been so manifest in our history and in our lives, and offering earnest prayers that His bounties may continue to us and to our children.

In witness whereof I have hereunto set my hand and caused the seal of the United States to be affixed.

Done at the city of Washington this fourth day of November in the year of our Lord one thousand eight hundred and eighty-one, and of the Independence of the United States the one hundred and sixth.

[SEAL.]   CHESTER A. ARTHUR.

By the President:

    JAMES G. BLAINE,

      Secretary of State.

MESSAGE

SENATE AND HOUSE OF REPRESENTATIVES

DECEMBER 6, 1881.

29

MESSAGE.

To the Senate and House of Representatives of the United States:

An appalling calamity has befallen the American people since their chosen representatives last met in the halls where you are now assembled. We might else recall with unalloyed content the rare prosperity with which throughout the year the nation has been blessed. Its harvests have been plenteous; its varied industries have thriven; the health of its people has been preserved; it has maintained with foreign Governments the undisturbed relations of amity and peace. For these manifestations of His favor, we owe to Him who holds our destiny in His hands the tribute of our grateful devotion.

To that mysterious exercise of His will, which has taken from us the loved and illustrious citizen who was but lately the head of the nation, we bow in sorrow and submission.

The memory of his exalted character, of his noble achievements, and of his patriotic life will be treasured forever as a sacred possession of the whole people.

The announcement of his death drew from foreign Governments and peoples tributes of sympathy and sorrow which history will record as signal tokens of the kinship of nations and the federation of mankind.

The feeling of good-will between our own Government and that of Great Britain was never more marked than at present. In recognition of this pleasing fact, I directed, on the occasion of the late centennial celebration at Yorktown, that a salute be given to the British flag.

Save for the correspondence to which I shall refer hereafter in relation to the proposed canal across the Isthmus of Panama, little has occurred worthy of mention in the diplomatic relations of the two countries.

Early in the year the Fortune Bay claims were satisfactorily settled by the British Government paying in full the sum of £15,000, most of which has been already distributed. As the terms of the settlement included compensation for injuries suffered by our fishermen at Aspee Bay, there has been retained from the gross award a sum which is deemed adequate for those claims.

The participation of Americans in the exhibitions at Melbourne and Sydney will be approvingly mentioned in the reports of the two exhibitions, soon to be presented to Congress. They will disclose the readiness of our countrymen to make successful competition in distant fields of enterprise.

Negotiations for an International Copyright Convention are in hopeful progress.

The surrender of Sitting Bull and his forces upon the Canadian frontier has allayed apprehension, although bodies of British Indians still cross the border in quest of sustenance. Upon this subject a correspondence has been opened, which promises an adequate understanding. Our troops have orders to avoid meanwhile all collisions with alien Indians.

The presence at the Yorktown celebration of representatives of the French Republic and descendants of Lafayette and of his gallant compatriots who were our allies in the Revolution, has served to strengthen the spirit of good-will which has always existed between the two nations.

You will be furnished with the proceedings of the Bi-metallic Conference held during the summer at the city of Paris. No accord was reached, but a valuable interchange of views was had, and the conference will next year be renewed.

At the Electrical Exhibition and Congress also held at Paris, this country was creditably represented by eminent specialists who, in the absence of an appropriation, generously lent their efficient aid at the instance of the State Department. While our exhibitors in this almost distinctively American field of achievement have won several valuable awards, I recommend that Congress provide for the repayment of the personal expenses incurred, in the public interest, by the honorary commissioners and delegates.

No new questions respecting the status of our naturalized citizens in Germany have arisen during the year, and the causes of complaint, especially in Alsace and Lorraine, have practically ceased through the liberal action of the Imperial Government in accepting our often-expressed views on the subject. The application of the treaty of 1868 to the lately acquired Rhenish provinces has received very earnest attention, and a definite and lasting agreement on this point is confidently expected. The participation of the descendants of Baron von Steuben in the Yorktown festivities, and their subsequent reception by their American kinsmen, strikingly evinced the ties of good-will which unite the German people and our own.

Our intercourse with Spain has been friendly. An agreement concluded in February last fixes a term for the labors of the Spanish and American Claims Commission. The Spanish Government has been requested to pay the late awards of that commission, and will, it is believed, accede to the request as promptly and courteously as on former occasions.

By recent legislation onerous fines have been imposed upon American shipping in Spanish and colonial ports for slight irregularities in manifests. One case of hardship is specially worthy of attention. The bark "Masonic," bound for Japan, entered Manila in distress, and is there sought to be confiscated under Spanish revenue laws for an alleged shortage in her trans-shipped cargo. Though efforts for her relief have thus far proved unavailing, it is expected that the whole matter will be adjusted in a friendly spirit.

The Senate resolutions of condolence on the assassination of the Czar Alexander II were appropriately communicated to the Russian Government, which in turn has expressed its sympathy in our late national bereavement. It is desirable that our cordial relations with Russia should be strengthened by proper engagements, assuring to peaceable Americans who visit the Empire the consideration which is due to them as citizens of a friendly state. This is especially needful with respect to American Israelites, whose classification with the native Hebrews has evoked energetic remonstrances from this Government.

3

A supplementary consular agreement with Italy has been sanctioned and proclaimed, which puts at rest conflicts of jurisdiction in the case of crimes on shipboard.

Several important international conferences have been held in Italy during the year. At the Geographical Congress of Venice, the Beneficence Congress of Milan, and the Hygienic Congress of Turin, this country was represented by delegates from branches of the public service, or by private citizens duly accredited in an honorary capacity. It is hoped that Congress will give such prominence to the results of their participation as they may seem to deserve.

The abolition of all discriminating duties against such colonial productions of the Dutch East Indies as are imported hither from Holland has been already considered by Congress. I trust that at the present session the matter may be favorably concluded.

The insecurity of life and property in many parts of Turkey has given rise to correspondence with the Porte, looking particularly to the better protection of American missionaries in the empire. The condemned murderer of the eminent missionary Dr. Justin W. Parsons has not yet been executed, although this Government has repeatedly demanded that exemplary justice be done.

The Swiss Government has again solicited the good offices of our diplomatic and consular agents for the protection of its citizens in countries where it is not itself represented. This request has, within proper limits, been granted.

Our agents in Switzerland have been instructed to protest against the conduct of the authorities of certain communes in permitting the emigration to this country of criminals and other ·objectionable persons. Several such persons, through the cooperation of the Commissioners of Emigration at New York, have been sent back by the steamers which brought them. A continuance of this course may prove a more effectual remedy than diplomatic remonstrance.

Treaties of commerce and navigation, and for the regulation of consular privileges, have been concluded with Roumania and Servia since their admission into the family of European states.

As is natural with contiguous states having like institutions and like aims of advancement and development, the friendship of the United States and Mexico has been constantly maintained. This

Government has lost no occasion of encouraging the Mexican Government to a beneficial realization of the mutual advantages which will result from more intimate commercial intercourse, and from the opening of the rich interior of Mexico to railway enterprise. I deem it important that means be provided to restrain the lawlessness unfortunately so common on the frontier, and to suppress the forays of the reservation Indians on either side of the Rio Grande.

The neighboring states of Central America have preserved internal peace, and their outward relations toward us have been those of intimate friendship. There are encouraging signs of their growing disposition to subordinate their local interests to those which are common to them by reason of their geographical relations.

The boundary dispute between Guatemala and Mexico has afforded this Government an opportunity to exercise its good offices for preventing a rupture between those states, and for procuring a peaceable solution of the question. I cherish strong hope that in view of our relations of amity with both countries our friendly counsels may prevail.

A special envoy of Guatemala has brought to me the condolences of his Government and people on the death of President Garfield.

The Costa Rican Government lately framed an engagement with Colombia for settling by arbitration the boundary question between those countries, providing that the post of arbitrator should be offered successively to the King of the Belgians, the King of Spain, and the President of the Argentine Confederation. The King of the Belgians has declined to act, but I am not as yet advised of the action of the King of Spain. As we have certain interests in the disputed territory which are protected by our treaty engagements with one of the parties, it is important that the arbitration should not, without our consent, affect our rights, and this Government has accordingly thought proper to make its views known to the parties to the agreement, as well as to intimate them to the Belgian and Spanish Governments.

The questions growing out of the proposed interoceanic waterway across the Isthmus of Panama are of grave national importance. This Government has not been unmindful of the solemn obligations imposed upon it by its compact of 1846 with Colombia, as the independent and sovereign mistress of the territory crossed by the canal, and has sought to render them effective by fresh engagements with the Colombian Republic looking to their practical execution. The negotiations to this end, after they had reached what appeared to be a mutually satisfactory solution here, were met in Colombia by a disavowal of the powers which its envoy had assumed, and by a proposal for renewed negotiation on a modified basis.

Meanwhile this Government learned that Colombia had proposed to the European powers to join in a guarantee of the neutrality of the proposed Panama Canal—a guarantee which would be in direct contravention of our obligation as the sole guarantor of the integrity of Colombian territory and of the neutrality of the canal itself. My lamented predecessor felt it his duty to place before the European powers the reasons which make the prior guarantee of the United States indispensable, and for which the interjection of any foreign guarantee might be regarded as a superfluous and unfriendly act.

Foreseeing the probable reliance of the British Government on the provisions of the Clayton-Bulwer treaty of 1850, as affording room for a share in the guarantees which the United States covenanted with Colombia four years before, I have not hesitated to supplement the action of my predecessor by proposing to Her Majesty's Government the modification of that instrument and the abrogation of such clauses thereof as do not comport with the obligations of the United States toward Colombia, or with the vital needs of the two friendly parties to the compact.

This Government sees with great concern the continuance of the hostile relations between Chili, Bolivia, and Peru. An early peace between these republics is much to be desired, not only that they may themselves be spared further misery and bloodshed, but because their continued antagonism threatens consequences which are, in my judgment, dangerous to the interests of republican government on this continent, and calculated to destroy the best elements of our free and peaceful civilization.

As in the present excited condition of popular feeling in these countries there has been serious misapprehension of the position of the United States, and as separate diplomatic intercourse with each through independent ministers is sometimes subject, owing to the want of prompt reciprocal communication, to temporary misunderstanding, I have deemed it judicious, at the present time, to send a special envoy, accredited to all and each of them, and furnished with general instructions, which will, I trust, enable him to bring these powers into friendly relations.

The Government of Venezuela maintains its attitude of warm friendship, and continues with great regularity its payment of the monthly quota of the diplomatic debt. Without suggesting the direction in which Congress should act, I ask its attention to the pending questions affecting the distribution of the sums thus far received.

The relations between Venezuela and France, growing out of the same debt, have been for some time past in an unsatisfactory state, and this Government, as the neighbor and one of the largest creditors of Venezuela, has interposed its influence with the French Government with the view of producing a friendly and honorable adjustment.

I regret that the commercial interests between the United States and Brazil, from which great advantages were hoped a year ago, have suffered from the withdrawal of the American lines of communication between the Brazilian ports and our own.

Through the efforts of our minister resident at Buenos Ayres and the United States minister at Santiago, a treaty has been concluded between the Argentine Republic and Chili, disposing of the long-pending Patagonian boundary question. It is a matter of congratulation that our Government has been afforded the opportunity of successfully exerting its good influence for the prevention of disagreements between these republics of the American continent.

I am glad to inform you that the treaties lately negotiated with China have been duly ratified on both sides, and the exchange made at Peking. Legislation is necessary to carry their provisions into effect. The prompt and friendly spirit with which the Chinese Government, at the request of the United States, conceded the modification of existing treaties, should secure careful regard for the interests and susceptibilities of that Government in the enactment of any laws relating to Chinese immigration.

Those clauses of the treaties which forbid the participation of citizens or vessels of the United States in the opium trade will doubtless receive your approval. They will attest the sincere interest which our people and Government feel in the commendable efforts of the Chinese Government to put a stop to this demoralizing and destructive traffic.

In relation both to China and Japan, some changes are desirable in our present system of consular jurisdiction. I hope at some future time to lay before you a scheme for its improvement in the entire East.

The intimacy between our own country and Japan, the most advanced of the eastern nations, continues to be cordial. I am advised that the Emperor contemplates the establishment of full constitutional government and that he has already summoned a parliamentary congress for the purpose of effecting the change. Such a remarkable step toward complete assimilation with the western system cannot fail to bring Japan into closer and more beneficial relationship with ourselves as the chief Pacific power.

A question has arisen in relation to the exercise in that country of the judicial functions conferred upon our ministers and consuls. The indictment, trial, and conviction in the consular court at Yokohama of John Ross, a merchant-seaman on board an American vessel, have made it necessary for the Government to institute a careful examination into the nature and methods of this jurisdiction.

It appeared that Ross was regularly shipped under the flag of the United States, but was by birth a British subject. My predecessor felt it his duty to maintain the position that, during his service as a regularly shipped seaman on board an American merchant vessel, Ross was subject to the laws of that service and to the jurisdiction of the United States consular authorities.

I renew the recommendation which has been heretofore urged by the Executive upon the attention of Congress, that after the reduction of such amount as may be found due to American citizens, the balance of the indemnity funds heretofore obtained from China and Japan, and which are now in the hands of the State Department, be returned to the Governments of those countries.

The King of Hawaii, in the course of his homeward return after a journey around the world, has lately visited this country. While our relations with that kingdom are friendly, this Government has viewed with concern the efforts to seek replenishment of the diminishing population of the islands from outward sources, to a degree which may impair the native sovereignty and independence, in which the United States was among the first to testify a lively interest.

Relations of unimpaired amity have been maintained throughout the year with the respective Governments of Austria-Hungary, Belgium, Denmark, Hayti, Paraguay and Uruguay, Portugal, and Sweden and Norway. This may also be said of Greece and Ecuador, although our relations with those states have for some years been severed by the withdrawal of appropriations for diplomatic representatives at Athens and Quito. It seems expedient to restore those missions, even on a reduced scale; and I decidedly recommend such a course with respect to Ecuador, which is likely, within the near future, to play an important part among the nations of the Southern Pacific.

At its last extra session the Senate called for the text of the Geneva Convention for the relief of the wounded in war. I trust that this action foreshadows such interest in the subject as will result in the adhesion of the United States to that humane and commendable engagement.

I invite your attention to the propriety of adopting the new Code of International Rules for the Prevention of Collisions on the high seas, and of conforming the domestic legislation of the United States thereto, so that no confusion may arise from the application of conflicting rules in the case of vessels of different nationalities meeting in tidal waters. These international rules differ but slightly from our own. They have been adopted by the Navy Department for the governance of the war ships of the United States on the high seas and in foreign waters; and, through the action of the State Department in disseminating the rules, and in acquainting shipmasters with the option of conforming to them without the jurisdictional waters of the United States, they are now very generally known and obeyed.

The State Department still continues to publish to the country the trade and manufacturing reports received from its officers abroad.

The success of this course warrants its continuance, and such appropriation as may be required to meet the rapidly-increasing demand for these publications. With special reference to the Atlanta Cotton Exposition, the October number of the reports was devoted to a valuable collection of papers on the cotton-goods trade of the world.

The International Sanitary Conference, for which, in 1879, Congress made provision, assembled in this city early in January last, and its sessions were prolonged until March. Although it reached no specific conclusions affecting the future action of the participant powers, the interchange of views proved to be most valuable. The full protocols of the sessions have been already presented to the Senate.

As pertinent to this general subject I call your attention to the operations of the National Board of Health. Established by act of Congress approved March 3, 1879, its sphere of duty was enlarged by the act of June 2 in the same year. By the last-named act the board was required to institute such measures as might be deemed necessary for preventing the introduction of contagious or infectious diseases from foreign countries into the United States or from one State into another.

The execution of the rules and regulations prepared by the board and approved by my predecessor has done much to arrest the progress of epidemic disease, and has thus rendered substantial service to the nation.

The International Sanitary Conference, to which I have referred, adopted a form of a bill of health to be used by all vessels seeking to enter the ports of the countries whose representatives participated in its deliberations. This form has since been prescribed by the National Board of Health and incorporated with its rules and regulations, which have been approved by me in pursuance of law.

The health of the people is of supreme importance. All measures looking to their protection against the spread of contagious diseases, and to the increase of our sanitary knowledge for such purposes, deserve attention of Congress.

The report of the Secretary of the Treasury presents in detail a highly satisfactory exhibit of the state of the finances and the condition of the various branches of the public service administered by that Department.

The ordinary revenues from all sources for the fiscal year ending June 30, 1881, were:

From customs	$198,159,676 02
From internal revenue.................................. :	135,264,385 51
From sales of public lands	2,201,863 17
From tax on circulation and deposits of national banks	8,116,115 72
From repayment of interest by Pacific Railway Companies	810,833 80
From sinking fund for Pacific Railway Companies	805,180 54
From customs fees, fines, penalties, &c	1,225,514 86
From fees—consular, letters patent, and lands	2,244,983 98
From proceeds of sales of Government property...	262,174 00
From profits on coinage	3,468,485 61
From revenues of the District of Columbia	2,016,199 23
From miscellaneous sources	6,206,880 13
Total ordinary receipts	360,782,292 57

The ordinary expenditures for the same period were:

For civil expenses.............	$17,941,177 19
For foreign intercourse	1,093,954 92
For Indians	6,514,161 09
For pensions....................................	50,059,279 62
For the military establishment, including river and harbor improvements and arsenals...................	40,466,460 55
For the naval establishment, including vessels, machinery, and improvements at navy-yards........	15,686,671 66
For miscellaneous expenditures, including public buildings, light-houses, and collecting the revenue	41,837,280 57
For expenditures on account of the District of Columbia..	3,543,912 03
For interest on the public debt	82,508,741 18
For premium on bonds purchased.............	1,061,248 78
Total ordinary expenditures.....................	260,712,887 59
Leaving a surplus revenue of	100,069,404 98

Which was applied as follows:

To the redemption of—

Bonds for the sinking fund	$74,371,200 00
Fractional currency for the sinking fund	109,001 05
Loan of February, 1861	7,418,000 00
Ten-forties of 1864..............	2,016,150 00
Five-twenties of 1862......................................	18,300 00
Five-twenties of 1864......................................	3,400 00
Five-twenties of 1865...........................	37,300 00
Consols of 1865	143,150 00
Consols of 1867......................................	959,150 00
Consols of 1868.................................	337,400 00
Texan indemnity stock	1,000 00
Old demand, compound-interest, and other notes ..	18,330 00
And to the increase of cash in the Treasury.........	14,637,023 93

100,069,404 98

The requirements of the sinking fund for the year amounted to $90,786,064.02, which sum included a balance of $49,817,128.78, not provided for during the previous fiscal year. The sum of $74,480,201.05 was applied to this fund, which left a deficit of $16,305,873.47. The increase of the revenues for 1881 over those of the previous year was $29,352,901.10. It is estimated that the receipts during the present fiscal year will reach $400,000,000, and the expenditures $270,000,000, leaving a surplus of $130,000,000 applicable to the sinking fund and the redemption of the public debt.

I approve the recommendation of the Secretary of the Treasury, that provision be made for the early retirement of silver certificates, and that the act requiring their issue be repealed. They were issued in pursuance of the policy of the Government to maintain silver at or near the gold standard, and were accordingly made receivable for all customs, taxes, and public dues. About sixty-six millions of them are now outstanding. They form an unnecessary addition to the paper currency, a sufficient amount of which may be readily supplied by the national banks.

In accordance with the act of February 28, 1878, the Treasury Department has, monthly, caused at least two millions in value of silver bullion to be coined into standard silver dollars. One hundred and two millions of these dollars have been already coined, while only about thirty-four millions are in circulation.

For the reasons which he specifies, I concur in the Secretary's recommendation that the provision for coinage of a fixed amount each month be repealed, and that hereafter only so much be coined as shall be necessary to supply the demand.

The Secretary advises that the issue of gold certificates should not for the present be resumed, and suggests that the national banks may properly be forbidden by law to retire their currency except upon reasonable notice of their intention so to do. Such legislation would seem to be justified by the recent action of certain banks on the occasion referred to in the Secretary's report.

Of the fifteen millions of fractional currency still outstanding, only about eighty thousand has been redeemed the past year. The suggestion that this amount may properly be dropped from future statements of the public debt seems worthy of approval.

So, also, does the suggestion of the Secretary as to the advisability of relieving the calendar of the United States courts in the southern district of New York, by the transfer to another tribunal of the numerous suits there pending against collectors.

The revenue from customs for the past fiscal year was $198,-159,676.02, an increase of $11,637,611.42 over that of the year preceding. $138,098,562.39 of this amount was collected at the port of New York, leaving $50,251,113.63 as the amount collected at all the other ports of the country. Of this sum, $47,977,137.63 was collected on sugar, melado, and molasses; $27,285,624.78 on wool and its manufactures; $21,462,534.34 on iron and steel, and manufactures thereof; $19,038,665.81 on manufactures of silk; $10,825,115.21 on manufactures of cotton; and $6,469,643.04 on wines and spirits; making a total revenue from these sources, of $133,058,720.81.

The expenses of collection for the past year were $6,419,345.20, an increase over the preceding year of $387,410.04. Notwithstanding the increase in the revenue from customs over the preceding year, the gross value of the imports, including free goods, decreased over twenty-five millions of dollars. The most marked decrease was in the value of unmanufactured wool, $14,023,682, and in that of scrap and pig iron, $12,810,671. The value of imported sugar, on the other hand, showed an increase of $7,457,474; of steel rails, $4,345,521; of barley, $2,154,204; and of steel in bars, ingots, &c., $1,620,046.

Contrasted with the imports during the last fiscal year, the exports were as follows:

Domestic merchandise..	$883,925,947
Foreign merchandise......	18,451,399
Total..................	902,377,346
Imports of merchandise........	642,664,628
Excess of exports over imports of merchandise..........	259,712,718
Aggregate of exports and imports..........................	1,545,041,974

Compared with the previous year, there was an increase of $66,-738,688 in the value of exports of merchandise, and a decrease of $25,290,118 in the value of imports. The annual average of the excess of imports of merchandise over exports thereof, for ten years previous to June 30, 1873, was $104,706,922; but for the last six years there has been an excess of exports over imports of merchandise amounting to $1,180,668,105, an annual average of $196,778,017. The specie value of the exports of domestic merchandise was $376,616,473 in 1870, and $883,925,947 in 1881, an increase of $507,309,474, or 135 per cent. The value of imports was $435,958,408 in 1870, and $642,664,628 in 1881, an increase of $206,706,220, or 47 per cent.

During each year from 1862 to 1879, inclusive, the exports of specie exceeded the imports. The largest excess of such exports over imports was reached during the year 1864, when it amounted to $92,280,929. But during the year ended June 30, 1880, the imports of coin and bullion exceeded the exports by $75,891,391; and during the last fiscal year the excess of imports over exports was $91,168,650.

In the last annual report of the Secretary of the Treasury the attention of Congress was called to the fact that $469,651,050 in five per centum bonds and $203,573,750 in six per centum bonds would become redeemable during the year, and Congress was asked to

authorize the refunding of these bonds at a lower rate of interest.
The bill for such refunding having failed to become a law, the Secretary of the Treasury, in April last, notified the holders of the
$195,690,400 six per centum bonds then outstanding, that the bonds
would be paid at par on the first day of July following, or that they
might be "continued" at the pleasure of the Government, to bear
interest at the rate of three and one-half per centum per annum.

Under this notice $178,055,150 of the six per centum bonds were
continued at the lower rate, and $17,635,250 were redeemed.

In the month of May a like notice was given respecting the redemption or continuance of the $439,841,350 of five per centum
bonds then outstanding, and of these, $401,504,900 were continued
at three and one-half per centum per annum, and $38,336,450
redeemed.

The six per centum bonds of the loan of February 8, 1861, and
of the Oregon war debt, amounting together to $14,125,800, having
matured during the year, the Secretary of the Treasury gave notice
of his intention to redeem the same, and such as have been presented have been paid from the surplus revenues. There have also
been redeemed at par $16,179,100 of the three and one-half per
centum "continued" bonds, making a total of bonds redeemed, or
which have ceased to bear interest during the year, of $123,969,650.

The reduction of the annual interest on the public debt through
these transactions is as follows:

By reduction of interest to three and one-half per
cent $10,473,952 25
By redemption of bonds 6,352,340 00

Total 16,826,292 25

The three and one-half per centum bonds, being payable at the
pleasure of the Government, are available for the investment of
surplus revenue without the payment of premiums.

Unless these bonds can be funded at a much lower rate of interest
than they now bear, I agree with the Secretary of the Treasury that
no legislation respecting them is desirable.

It is a matter for congratulation that the business of the country
has been so prosperous during the past year as to yield by taxation

a large surplus of income to the Government. If the revenue laws remain unchanged this surplus must, year by year, increase, on account of the reduction of the public debt and its burden of interest, and because of the rapid increase of our population. In 1860, just prior to the institution of our internal-revenue system, our population but slightly exceeded 30,000,000; by the census of 1880 it is now found to exceed 50,000,000. It is estimated that even if the annual receipts and expenditures should continue as at present the entire debt could be paid in ten years.

In view, however, of the heavy load of taxation which our people have already borne, we may well consider whether it is not the part of wisdom to reduce the revenues, even if we delay a little the payment of the debt.

It seems to me that the time has arrived when the people may justly demand some relief from their present onerous burden, and that by due economy in the various branches of the public service, this may readily be afforded.

I therefore concur with the Secretary in recommending the abolition of all internal-revenue taxes, except those upon tobacco in its various forms, and upon distilled spirits and fermented liquors; and except also the special tax upon the manufacturers of, and dealers in,, such articles. The retention of the latter tax is desirable as affording the officers of the Government a proper supervision of these articles for the prevention of fraud. I agree with the Secretary of the Treasury, that the law imposing a stamp tax upon matches, proprietary articles, playing cards, checks, and drafts, may with propriety be repealed, and the law also by which banks and bankers are assessed upon their capital and deposits. There seems to be a general sentiment in favor of this course.

In the present condition of our revenues the tax upon deposits is especially unjust. It was never imposed in this country until it was demanded by the necessities of war, and was never exacted, I believe, in any other country, even in its greatest exigencies. Banks are required to secure their circulation by pledging with the Treasurer of the United States bonds of the General Government. The interest upon these bonds, which at the time when the tax was imposed was 6 per cent., is now, in most instances, 3½ per cent. Besides, the entire circulation was originally limited by law and no increase was allowable. When the existing banks had practically a monopoly of the business, there was force in the suggestion, that for the franchise to the favored grantees the Government might very properly exact a tax on circulation; but for years the system has been free, and the amount of circulation regulated by the public demand.

The retention of this tax has been suggested as a means of reimbursing the Government for the expense of printing and furnishing the circulating notes. If the tax should be repealed it would certainly seem proper to require the national banks to pay the amount of such expense to the Comptroller of the Currency.

It is perhaps doubtful whether the immediate reduction of the rate of taxation upon liquors and tobacco is advisable, especially in view of the drain upon the Treasury which must attend the payment of arrears of pensions. A comparison, however, of the amount of taxes collected under the varying rates of taxation which have at different times prevailed, suggests the intimation that some reduction may soon be made without material diminution of the revenue.

The tariff laws also need revision ; but, that a due regard may be paid to the conflicting interests of our citizens, important changes should be made with caution. If a careful revision cannot be made at this session, a commission such as was lately approved by the Senate and is now recommended by the Secretary of the Treasury would doubtless lighten the labors of Congress whenever this subject shall be brought to its consideration.

The accompanying report of the Secretary of War will make known to you the operations of that Department for the past year.

He suggests measures for promoting the efficiency of the Army without adding to the number of its officers, and recommends the legislation necessary to increase the number of enlisted men to thirty thousand, the maximum allowed by law.

This he deems necessary to maintain quietude on our ever-shifting frontier; to preserve peace and suppress disorder and marauding in new settlements; to protect settlers and their property against Indians, and Indians against the encroachments of intruders; and to enable peaceable immigrants to establish homes in the most remote parts of our country.

The Army is now necessarily scattered over such a vast extent of territory that, whenever an outbreak occurs, reinforcements must be hurried from many quarters, over great distances, and always at heavy cost for transportation of men, horses, wagons, and supplies.

I concur in the recommendations of the Secretary for increasing the Army to the strength of thirty thousand enlisted men.

It appears by the Secretary's report that in the absence of disturbances on the frontier the troops have been actively employed in collecting the Indians hitherto hostile, and locating them on their proper reservations; that Sitting Bull and his adherents are now prisoners at Fort Randall; that the Utes have been moved to their new reservation in Utah; that during the recent outbreak of the Apaches it was necessary to reinforce the garrisons in Arizona by troops withdrawn from New Mexico; and that some of the Apaches are now held prisoners for trial, while some have escaped, and the majority of the tribe are now on their reservation.

There is need of legislation to prevent intrusion upon the lands set apart for the Indians. A large military force, at great expense, is now required to patrol the boundary line between Kansas and the Indian Territory. The only punishment that can at present be inflicted is the forcible removal of the intruder and the imposition of a pecuniary fine, which, in most cases, it is impossible to collect. There should be a penalty by imprisonment in such cases.

The separate organization of the Signal Service is urged by the Secretary of War, and a full statement of the advantages of such permanent organization is presented in the report of the Chief Signal Officer. A detailed account of the useful work performed by the Signal Corps and the Weather Bureau, is also given in that report.

I ask attention to the statements of the Secretary of War regarding the requisitions frequently made by the Indian Bureau upon the Subsistence Department of the Army for the casual support of bands and tribes of Indians whose appropriations are exhausted. The War Department should not be left, by reason of inadequate provision for the Indian Bureau, to contribute for the maintenance of Indians.

The report of the Chief of Engineers furnishes a detailed account of the operations for the improvement of rivers and harbors.

I commend to your attention the suggestions contained in this report in regard to the condition of our fortifications, especially our coast defenses, and recommend an increase of the strength of the Engineer Battalion, by which the efficiency of our torpedo system would be improved.

I also call your attention to the remarks upon the improvement of the South Pass of the Mississippi River, the proposed free bridge over the Potomac River at Georgetown, the importance of completing at an early day the north wing of the War Department building, and other recommendations of the Secretary of War which appear in his report.

The actual expenditures of that Department for the fiscal year ending June 30, 1881, were $42,122,201.39. The appropriations for the year 1882 were $44,889,725.42. The estimates for 1883 are $44,541,276.91.

The report of the Secretary of the Navy exhibits the condition of that branch of the service, and presents valuable suggestions for its improvement. I call your especial attention also to the appended report of the Advisory Board, which he convened to devise suitable measures for increasing the efficiency of the Navy, and particularly to report as to the character and number of vessels necessary to place it upon a footing commensurate with the necessities of the Government.

I cannot too strongly urge upon you my conviction that every consideration of national safety, economy, and honor imperatively demands a thorough rehabilitation of our Navy.

With a full appreciation of the fact that compliance with the suggestions of the head of that Department and of the Advisory Board must involve a large expenditure of the public moneys, I earnestly recommend such appropriations as will accomplish an end which seems to me so desirable.

Nothing can be more inconsistent with true public economy than withholding the means necessary to accomplish the objects intrusted by the Constitution to the national legislature. One of those objects, and one which is of paramount importance, is declared by our fundamental law to be the provision for the "common defense." Surely nothing is more essential to the defense of the United States and of all our people than the efficiency of our Navy.

4*

We have for many years maintained with foreign Governments the relations of honorable peace, and that such relations may be permanent is desired by every patriotic citizen of the Republic.

But if we heed the teachings of history we shall not forget that in the life of every nation emergencies may arise when a resort to arms can alone save it from dishonor.

No danger from abroad now threatens this people, nor have we any cause to distrust the friendly professions of other Governments. But for avoiding as well as for repelling dangers that may threaten us in the future, we must be prepared to enforce any policy which we think wise to adopt.

We must be ready to defend our harbors against aggression, to protect, by the distribution of our ships of war over the highways of commerce, the varied interests of our foreign trade, and the persons and property of our citizens abroad, to maintain everywhere the honor of our flag, and the distinguished position which we may rightfully claim among the nations of the world.

The report of the Postmaster-General is a gratifying exhibit of the growth and efficiency of the postal service.

The receipts from postage and other ordinary sources during the past fiscal year were $36,489,816.58. The receipts from the money-order business were $295,581.39, making a total of $36,785,397.97. The expenditure for the fiscal year was $39,251,736.46. The deficit supplied out of the general Treasury was $2,481,129.35, or $6\frac{3}{10}$ per cent. of the amount expended. The receipts were $3,469,918.63 in excess of those of the previous year, and $4,575,397.97 in excess of the estimate made two years ago, before the present period of business prosperity had fairly begun.

The whole number of letters mailed in this country in the last fiscal year exceeded one thousand millions.

The registry system is reported to be in excellent condition, having been remodeled during the past four years, with good results. The amount of registration fees collected during the last fiscal year was $712,882.20, an increase over the fiscal year ending June 30, 1877, of $345,443.40.

The entire number of letters and packages registered during the year was 8,338,919, of which only 2,061 were lost or destroyed in transit.

The operations of the money-order system are multiplying yearly under the impulse of immigration, of the rapid development of the newer States and Territories, and the consequent demand for additional means of intercommunication and exchange.

During the past year, 338 additional money-order offices have been established, making a total of 5,499 in operation at the date of this report.

During the year the domestic money orders aggregated in value $105,075,769.35.

A modification of the system is suggested, reducing the fees for money orders not exceeding $5 from ten cents to five cents, and making the maximum limit $100 in place of $50.

Legislation for the disposition of unclaimed money orders in the possession of the Post-Office Department is recommended, in view of the fact that their total value now exceeds one million dollars.

The attention of Congress is again invited to the subject of establishing a system of savings depositories in connection with the Post-Office Department.

The statistics of mail transportation show that during the past year railroad routes have been increased in length 6,249 miles, and in cost $1,114,382, while steamboat routes have been decreased in length 2,182 miles, and in cost $134,054. The so-called star routes have been decreased in length 3,949 miles, and in cost $364,144.

Nearly all of the more expensive routes have been superseded by railroad service. The cost of the star service must therefore rapidly decrease in the Western States and Territories.

The Postmaster-General, however, calls attention to the constantly increasing cost of the railway mail service as a serious difficulty in the way of making the Department self-sustaining.

Our postal intercourse with foreign countries has kept pace with the growth of the domestic service. Within the past year several countries and colonies have declared their adhesion to the Postal Union. It now includes all those which have an organized postal service, except Bolivia, Costa Rica, New Zealand, and the British colonies in Australia.

As has been already stated, great reductions have recently been made in the expense of the star-route service. The investigations of the Department of Justice and the Post-Office Department have resulted in the presentation of indictments against persons formerly connected with that service, accusing them of offenses against the United States. I have enjoined upon the officials who are charged with the conduct of the cases on the part of the Government and upon the eminent counsel who, before my accession to the Presidency, were called to their assistance, the duty of prosecuting with the utmost vigor of the law all persons who may be found chargeable with frauds upon the postal service.

The Acting Attorney-General calls attention to the necessity of modifying the present system of the courts of the United States—a necessity due to the large increase of business, especially in the Supreme Court. Litigation in our Federal tribunals became greatly expanded after the close of the late war. So long as that expansion might be attributable to the abnormal condition in which the community found itself immediately after the return of peace, prudence required that no change be made in the constitution of our judicial tribunals.

But it has now become apparent that an immense increase of litigation has directly resulted from the wonderful growth and development of the country. There is no ground for belief that the business of the United States courts will ever be less in volume than at present. Indeed, that it is likely to be much greater is generally recognized by the bench and bar.

In view of the fact that Congress has already given much consideration to this subject, I make no suggestion as to detail, but express the hope that your deliberations may result in such legislation as will give early relief to our overburdened courts.

The Acting Attorney-General also calls attention to the disturbance of the public tranquillity during the past year in the Territory of Arizona. A band of armed desperadoes, known as "Cow Boys," probably numbering from fifty to one hundred men, have been engaged for months in committing acts of lawlessness and brutality which the local authorities have been unable to repress. The depredations of these "Cow Boys" have also extended into Mexico, which the marauders reach from the Arizona frontier. With every disposition to meet the exigencies of the case, I am embarrassed by lack of authority to deal with them effectually. The punishment of crimes committed within Arizona should ordinarily, of course, be left to the Territorial authorities. But it is worthy consideration whether acts which necessarily tend to embroil the United States with neighboring Governments should not be declared crimes against the United States. Some of the incursions alluded to may perhaps be within the scope of the law (Revised Statutes, section 5286) forbidding "military expeditions or enterprises" against friendly states; but in view of the speedy assembling of your body, I have preferred to await such legislation as in your wisdom the occasion may seem to demand.

It may, perhaps, be thought proper to provide that the setting on foot within our own territory, of brigandage and armed marauding expeditions against friendly nations and their citizens, shall be punishable as an offense against the United States.

I will add that in the event of a request from the Territorial government for protection by the United States against "domestic violence," this Government would be powerless to render assistance.

The act of 1795, chapter 36, passed at a time when Territorial governments received little attention from Congress, enforced this duty of the United States only as to the State governments. But the act of 1807, chapter 39, applied also to Territories. This law seems to have remained in force until the revision of the statutes, when the provision for the Territories was dropped. I am not advised whether this alteration was intentional or accidental, but, as it seems to me that the Territories should be offered the protection which is accorded to the States by the Constitution, I suggest legislation to that end.

It seems to me, too, that whatever views may prevail as to the policy of recent legislation by which the Army has ceased to be a part of the *posse comitatus*, an exception might well be made for permitting the military to assist the civil Territorial authorities in enforcing the laws of the United States. This use of the Army would not seem to be within the alleged evil against which that legislation was aimed. From sparseness of population and other circumstances it is often quite impracticable to summon a civil posse in places where officers of justice require assistance, and where a military force is within easy reach.

The report of the Secretary of the Interior, with accompanying documents, presents an elaborate account of the business of that Department. A summary of it would be too extended for this place. I ask your careful attention to the report itself.

Prominent among the matters which challenge the attention of Congress at its present session is the management of our Indian affairs. While this question has been a cause of trouble and embarrassment from the infancy of the Government, it is but recently that any effort has been made for its solution, at once serious, determined, consistent, and promising success.

It has been easier to resort to convenient makeshifts for tiding over temporary difficulties than to grapple with the great permanent problem, and, accordingly, the easier course has almost invariably been pursued.

It was natural, at a time when the national territory seemed almost illimitable and contained many millions of acres far outside the bounds of civilized settlements, that a policy should have been initiated which more than aught else has been the fruitful source of our Indian complications.

I refer of course to the policy of dealing with the various Indian tribes as separate nationalities, of relegating them by treaty stipulations to the occupancy of immense reservations in the West, and of encouraging them to live a savage life, undisturbed by any earnest and well-directed efforts to bring them under the influences of civilization.

The unsatisfactory results which have sprung from this policy are becoming apparent to all.

As the white settlements have crowded the borders of the reservations, the Indians, sometimes contentedly and sometimes against their will, have been transferred to other hunting-grounds, from which they have again been dislodged whenever their new-found homes have been desired by the adventurous settlers.

These removals, and the frontier collisions by which they have often been preceded, have led to frequent and disastrous conflicts between the races.

It is profitless to discuss here which of them has been chiefly responsible for the disturbances whose recital occupies so large a space upon the pages of our history.

We have to deal with the appalling fact that though thousands of lives have been sacrificed, and hundreds of millions of dollars expended in the attempt to solve the Indian problem, it has until within the past few years seemed scarcely nearer a solution than it was half a century ago.   But the Government has of late been cautiously but steadily feeling its way to the adoption of a policy which has already produced gratifying results, and which, in my judgment, is likely, if Congress and the Executive accord in its support, to relieve us ere long from the difficulties which have hitherto beset us.

For the success of the efforts now making to introduce among the Indians the customs and pursuits of civilized life, and gradually to absorb them into the mass of our citizens, sharing their rights and holden to their responsibilities, there is imperative need for legislative action.

My suggestions in that regard will be chiefly such as have been already called to the attention of Congress, and have received to some extent its consideration:

First. I recommend the passage of an act making the laws of the various States and Territories applicable to the Indian reservations within their borders, and extending the laws of the State of Arkansas to the portion of the Indian Territory not occupied by the five civilized tribes.

The Indian should receive the protection of the law.   He should be allowed to maintain in court his rights of person and property. He has repeatedly begged for this privilege.   Its exercise would be very valuable to him in his progress toward civilization.

Second. Of even greater importance is a measure which has been frequently recommended by my predecessors in office, and in furtherance of which several bills have been from time to time introduced in both Houses of Congress.   The enactment of a general law permitting the allotment in severalty, to such Indians, at least, as desire it, of a reasonable quantity of land secured to them by patent, and for their own protection made inalienable for twenty or twenty-five years, is demanded for their present welfare and their permanent advancement.

In return for such considerate action on the part of the Government, there is reason to believe that the Indians in large numbers would be persuaded to sever their tribal relations and to engage at once in agricultural pursuits. Many of them realize the fact that their hunting days are over, and that it is now for their best interests to conform their manner of life to the new order of things. By no greater inducement than the assurance of permanent title to the soil can they be led to engage in the occupation of tilling it.

The well-attested reports of their increasing interest in husbandry justify the hope and belief that the enactment of such a statute as I recommend would be at once attended with gratifying results. A resort to the allotment system would have a direct and powerful influence in dissolving the tribal bond, which is so prominent a feature of savage life, and which tends so strongly to perpetuate it.

Third. I advise a liberal appropriation for the support of Indian schools, because of my confident belief that such a course is consistent with the wisest economy.

Even among the most uncultivated Indian tribes there is reported to be a general and urgent desire on the part of the chiefs and older members for the education of their children. It is unfortunate, in view of this fact, that during the past year the means which have been at the command of the Interior Department for the purpose of Indian instruction have proved to be utterly inadequate.. The success of the schools which are in operation at Hampton, Carlisle, and Forest Grove should not only encourage a more generous provision for the support of those institutions, but should prompt the establishment of others of a similar character.

They are doubtless much more potent for good than the day schools upon the reservation, as the pupils are altogether separated from the surroundings of savage life, and brought into constant contact with civilization.

There are many other phases of this subject which are of great interest, but which cannot be included within the becoming limits of this communication; they are discussed ably in the reports of the Secretary of the Interior and the Commissioner of Indian Affairs.

For many years the Executive, in his annual message to Congress, has urged the necessity of stringent legislation for the suppression of polygamy in the Territories, and especially in the Territory of Utah. The existing statute for the punishment of this odious crime, so revolting to the moral and religious sense of.Christendom, has been persistently and contemptuously violated ever since its enactment. Indeed, in spite of commendable efforts on the part of the authorities who represent the United States in that Territory, the law has in very rare instances been enforced, and, for a cause to which reference will presently be made, is practically a dead letter.

The fact that adherents of the Mormon church, which rests upon polygamy as its corner-stone, have recently been peopling in large numbers Idaho, Arizona, and other of our Western Territories, is well calculated to excite the liveliest interest and apprehension. It imposes upon Congress and the Executive the duty of arraying against this barbarous system all the power which, under the Constitution and the law, they can wield for its destruction.

Reference has been already made to the obstacles which the United States officers have encountered in their efforts to punish violations of law. Prominent among these obstacles is the difficulty of procuring legal evidence sufficient to warrant a conviction even in the case of the most notorious offenders.

Your attention is called to a recent opinion of the Supreme Court of the United States, explaining its judgment of reversal in the case of Miles, who had· been convicted of bigamy in Utah. The court refers to the fact that the secrecy attending the celebration of marriages in that Territory makes the proof of polygamy very difficult; and the propriety is suggested of modifying the law of evidence which now makes a wife incompetent to testify against her husband.

This suggestion is approved. I recommend also the passage of an act providing that in the Territories of the United States the fact that a woman has been married to a person charged with bigamy shall not disqualify her as a witness upon his trial for that offense. I further recommend legislation by which any person solemnizing a marriage in any of the Territories shall be required, under stringent penalties for neglect or refusal, to file a certificate of such marriage in the supreme court of the Territory.

Doubtless Congress may devise other practicable measures for obviating the difficulties which have hitherto attended the efforts to suppress this iniquity. I assure you of my determined purpose to co-operate with you in any lawful and discreet measures which may be proposed to that end.

Although our system of government does not contemplate that the nation should provide or support a system for the education of our people, no measures calculated to promote that general intelligence and virtue upon which the perpetuity of our institutions so greatly depends, have ever been regarded with indifference by Congress or the Executive.

A large portion of the public domain has been, from time to time, devoted to the promotion of education.

There is now a special reason why, by setting apart the proceeds of its sales of public lands, or by some other course, the Government should aid the work of education. Many who now exercise the right of suffrage are unable to read the ballot which they cast. Upon many who had just emerged from a condition of slavery, were suddenly devolved the responsibilities of citizenship in that portion of the country most impoverished by war. I have been pleased to learn from the report of the Commissioner of Education that there has lately been a commendable increase of interest and effort for their instruction; but all that can be done by local legislation and private generosity should be supplemented by such aid as can be constitutionally afforded by the National Government.

I would suggest that if any fund be dedicated to this purpose it may be wisely distributed in the different States according to the ratio of illiteracy, as by this means those localities which are most in need of such assistance will reap its special benefits.

The report of the Commissioner of Agriculture exhibits the results of the experiments in which that Department has been engaged during the past year, and makes important suggestions in reference to the agricultural development of the country.

The steady increase of our population, and the consequent addition to the number of those engaging in the pursuit of husbandry, are giving to this Department a growing dignity and importance. The Commissioner's suggestions touching its capacity for greater usefulness deserve attention, as it more and more commends itself to the interests which it was created to promote.

It appears from the report of the Commissioner of Pensions that, since 1860, 789,063 original pension claims have been filed; 450,949 of these have been allowed and inscribed on the pension-roll; 72,539 have been rejected and abandoned, being 13+ per cent. of the whole number of claims settled.

There are now pending for settlement 265,575 original pension claims, 227,040 of which were filed prior to July 1, 1880. These, when allowed, will involve the payment of arrears from the date of discharge in case of an invalid, and from date of death or termination of a prior right in all other cases.

From all the data obtainable it is estimated that 15 per cent. of the number of claims now pending will be rejected or abandoned. This would show the probable rejection of 34,040 cases, and the probable admission of about 193,000 claims, all of which involve the payment of arrears of pensions.

With the present force employed, the number of adjudications remaining the same and no new business intervening, this number of claims (193,000) could be acted upon in a period of six years; and taking January 1, 1884, as a near period from which to estimate in each case an average amount of arrears, it is found that every case allowed would require, for the first payment upon it, the sum of $1,350. Multiplying this amount by the whole number of probable admissions gives $250,000,000 as the sum required for first payments. This represents the sum which must be paid upon claims which were filed before July 1, 1880, and are now pending, and entitled to the benefits of the arrears act. From this amount ($250,000,000) may be deducted from ten to fifteen millions, for cases where, the claimant dying, there is no person who, under the law, would be entitled to succeed to the pension, leaving $235,000,000 as the probable amount to be paid.

In these estimates, no account has been taken of the 38,500 cases filed since June 30, 1880, and now pending, which must receive attention as current business, but which do not involve the payment of any arrears beyond the date of filing the claim. Of this number it is estimated that 86 per cent. will be allowed.

As has been stated, with the present force of the Pension Bureau, 675 clerks, it is estimated that it will take six years to dispose of the claims now pending.

It is stated by the Commissioner of Pensions that by an addition of 250 clerks (increasing the adjudicating force rather than the mechanical) double the amount of work could be accomplished, so that these cases could be acted upon within three years.

Aside from the considerations of justice which may be urged for a speedy settlement of the claims now on the files of the Pension Office, it is no less important on the score of economy, inasmuch as fully one-third of the clerical force of the office is now wholly occupied in giving attention to correspondence with the thousands of claimants whose cases have been on the files for the past eighteen years. The fact that a sum so enormous must be expended by the Government to meet demands for arrears of pensions, is an admonition to Congress and the Executive to give cautious consideration to any similar project in the future. The great temptation to the presentation of fictitious claims afforded by the fact that the average sum obtained upon each application is $1,300, leads me to suggest the propriety of making some special appropriation for the prevention of fraud.

I advise appropriations for such internal improvements as the wisdom of Congress may deem to be of public importance. The necessity of improving the navigation of the Mississippi River justifies a special allusion to that subject. I suggest the adoption of some measure for the removal of obstructions which now impede the navigation of that great channel of commerce.

In my letter accepting the nomination for the Vice-Presidency, I stated that in my judgment "no man should be the incumbent of an office, the duties of which he is for any cause unfit to perform; who is lacking in the ability, fidelity, or integrity which a proper administration of such office demands. This sentiment would doubtless meet with general acquiescence, but opinion has been widely divided upon the wisdom and practicability of the various reformatory schemes which have been suggested and of certain proposed regulations governing appointments to public office.

"The efficiency of such regulations has been distrusted, mainly because they have seemed to exalt mere educational and abstract tests above general business capacity and even special fitness for the particular work in hand. It seems to me that the rules which should be applied to the management of the public service, may properly conform in the main to such as regulate the conduct of successful private business:

"Original appointments should be based upon ascertained fitness.

"The tenure of office should be stable.

"Positions of responsibility should, so far as practicable, be filled by the promotion of worthy and efficient officers.

"The investigation of all complaints and the punishment of all official misconduct should be prompt and thorough."

The views expressed in the foregoing letter are those which will govern my administration of the Executive Office. They are doubtless shared by all intelligent and patriotic citizens, however divergent in their opinions as to the best methods of putting them into practical operation.

For example, the assertion that "original appointments should be based upon ascertained fitness" is not open to dispute.

But the question how in practice such fitness can be most effectually ascertained, is one which has for years excited interest and discussion. The measure, which, with slight variations in its details, has lately been urged upon the attention of Congress and the Executive, has as its principal feature the scheme of competitive examination. Save for certain exceptions, which need not here be specified, this plan would allow admission to the service only in its lowest grade, and would accordingly demand that all vacancies in higher positions should be filled by promotion alone. In these particulars it is in conformity with the existing civil-service system of Great Britain. And indeed the success which has attended that system in the country of its birth is the strongest argument which has been urged for its adoption here.

The fact should not, however, be overlooked that there are certain features of the English system which have not generally been received with favor in this country, even among the foremost advocates of civil-service reform.

Among them are :

1. A tenure of office which is substantially a life-tenure.

2. A limitation of the maximum age at which an applicant can enter the service, whereby all men in middle life or older, are, with some exceptions, rigidly excluded.

3. A retiring allowance upon going out of office.

These three elements are as important factors of the problem as any of the others. To eliminate them from the English system would effect a most radical change in its theory and practice.

The avowed purpose of that system is to induce the educated young men of the country to devote their lives to public employment by an assurance that having once entered upon it they need never leave it, and that after voluntary retirement they shall be the recipients of an annual pension. That this system as an entirety has proved very successful in Great Britain seems to be generally conceded even by those who once opposed its adoption.

To a statute which should incorporate all its essential features, I should feel bound to give my approval. But whether it would be for the best interests of the public to fix upon an expedient for immediate and extensive application, which embraces certain features of the English system but excludes or ignores others of equal importance, may be seriously doubted, even by those who are impressed, as I am myself, with the grave importance of correcting the evils which inhere in the present methods of appointment.

If, for example, the English rule which shuts out persons above the age of twenty-five years from a large number of public employments is not to be made an essential part of our own system, it is questionable whether the attainment of the highest number of marks at a competitive examination should be the criterion by which all applications for appointment should be put to test. And under similar conditions, it may also be questioned, whether admission to the service should be strictly limited to its lowest ranks.

There are very many characteristics which go to make a model civil servant. Prominent among them are probity, industry, good sense, good habits, good temper, patience, order, courtesy, tact, self-reliance, manly deference to superior officers and manly consideration for inferiors. The absence of these traits is not supplied by wide knowledge of books or by promptitude in answering questions, or by any other quality likely to be brought to light by competitive examination.

To make success in such a contest, therefore, an indispensable condition of public employment, would very likely result in the practical exclusion of the older applicants, even though they might possess qualifications far superior to their younger and more brilliant competitors.

These suggestions must not be regarded as evincing any spirit of opposition to the competitive plan, which has been to some extent successfully employed already, and which may hereafter vindicate the claim of its most earnest supporters. But it ought to be seriously considered whether the application of the same educational standard to persons of mature years and to young men fresh from school and college would not be likely to exalt mere intellectual proficiency above other qualities of equal or greater importance.

Another feature of the proposed system is the selection by promotion of all officers of the Government above the lowest grade, except such as would fairly be regarded as exponents of the policy of the Executive and the principles of the dominant party.

To afford encouragement to faithful public servants by exciting in their minds the hope of promotion, if they are found to merit it, is much to be desired.

But would it be wise to adopt a rule so rigid as to permit no other mode of supplying the intermediate walks of the service ?

There are many persons who fill subordinate positions with great credit, but lack those qualities which are requisite for higher posts of duty; and, besides, the modes of thought and action of one whose service in a governmental bureau has been long continued are often so cramped by routine procedure as almost to disqualify him from instituting changes required by the public interests. An infusion of new blood, from time to time, into the middle ranks of the service might be very beneficial in its results.

The subject under discussion is one of grave importance. The evils which are complained of cannot be eradicated at once; the work must be gradual.

The present English system is a growth of years, and was not created by a single stroke of executive or legislative action.

Its beginnings are found in an order in council, promulgated in 1855, and it was after patient and cautious scrutiny of its workings that fifteen years later it took its present shape.

Five years after the issuance of the order in council, and at a time when resort had been had to competitive examinations as an experiment much more extensively than has yet been the case in this country, a select committee of the House of Commons made a report to that house, which, declaring its approval of the competitive plan, deprecated, nevertheless, any precipitancy in its general adoption as likely to endanger its ultimate success.

During this tentative period the results of the two methods of pass examination and competitive examination were closely watched and compared. It may be that before we confine ourselves upon this important question within the stringent bounds of statutory enactment, we may profitably await the result of further inquiry and experiment.

The submission of a portion of the nominations to a central board of examiners selected solely for testing the qualifications of applicants may, perhaps, without resort to the competitive test, put an end to the mischiefs which attend the present system of appointment, and it may be feasible to vest in such a board a wide discretion to ascertain the characteristics and attainments of candidates in those particulars which I have already referred to as being no less important than mere intellectual attainment.

If Congress should deem it advisable at the present session to establish competitive tests for admission to the service, no doubts such as have been suggested shall deter me from giving the measure my earnest support.

And I urgently recommend, should there be a failure to pass any other act upon this subject, that an appropriation of $25,000 per year may be made for the enforcement of section 1753 of the Revised Statutes.

With the aid thus afforded me, I shall strive to execute the provisions of that law according to its letter and spirit.

I am unwilling, in justice to the present civil servants of the

Government, to dismiss this subject without declaring my dissent from the severe and almost indiscriminate censure with which they have been recently assailed. That they are as a class indolent, inefficient, and corrupt, is a statement which has been often made and widely credited. But when the extent, variety, delicacy, and importance of their duties are considered, the great majority of the employés of the Government are in my judgment deserving of high commendation.

The continuing decline of the merchant marine of the United States is greatly to be deplored. In view of the fact that we furnish so large a proportion of the freights of the commercial world and that our shipments are steadily and rapidly increasing, it is cause of surprise that not only is our navigation interest diminishing, but it is less than when our exports and imports were not half so large as now, either in bulk or value. There must be some peculiar hinderance to the development of this interest, or the enterprise and energy of American mechanics and capitalists would have kept this country at least abreast of our rivals in the friendly contest for ocean supremacy. The substitution of iron for wood and of steam for sail have wrought great revolutions in the carrying trade of the world; but these changes could not have been adverse to America if we had given to our navigation interests a portion of the aid and protection which have been so wisely bestowed upon our manufactures. I commend the whole subject to the wisdom of Congress, with the suggestion that no question of greater magnitude or farther-reaching importance can engage their attention.

In 1875 the Supreme Court of the United States declared unconstitutional the statutes of certain States which imposed upon ship-owners or consignees a tax of one dollar and a half for each passenger arriving from a foreign country, or, in lieu thereof, required a bond to indemnify the State and local authorities against expense for the future relief or support of such passenger. Since this decision the expense attending the care and supervision of immigrants has fallen on the States at whose ports they have landed. As a large majority of such immigrants, immediately upon their arrival, proceed to the inland States and the Territories to seek permanent homes, it is manifestly unjust to impose upon the State whose shores they first reach, the burden which it now bears. For this reason, and because of the national importance of the subject, I recommend legislation regarding the supervision and transitory care of immigrants at the ports of debarkation.

I regret to state that the people of Alaska have reason to complain that they are as yet unprovided with any form of government by which life or property can be protected. While the extent of its population does not justify the application of the costly machinery of Territorial administration, there is immediate necessity for constituting such a form of government as will promote the education of the people and secure the administration of justice.

The Senate, at its last session, passed a bill providing for the construction of a building for the Library of Congress, but it failed to become a law. The provision of suitable protection for this great collection of books, and for the copyright department connected with it, has become a subject of national importance and should receive prompt attention.

The report of the Commissioners of the District of Columbia, herewith transmitted, will inform you fully of the condition of the affairs of the District.

They urge the vital importance of legislation for the reclamation and improvement of the marshes and for the establishment of the harbor lines along the Potomac River front.

It is represented that in their present condition these marshes seriously affect the health of the residents of the adjacent parts of the city; and that they greatly mar the general aspect of the park in which stands the Washington Monument. This improvement would add to that park and to the park south of the Executive Mansion a large area of valuable land, and would transform what is now believed to be a dangerous nuisance into an attractive landscape extending to the river front.

They recommend the removal of the steam railway lines from the surface of the streets of the city, and the location of the necessary depots in such places as may be convenient for the public accommodation; and they call attention to the deficiency of the water supply, which seriously affects the material prosperity of the city and the health and comfort of its inhabitants.

I commend these subjects to your favorable consideration.

The importance of timely legislation with respect to the ascertainment and declaration of the vote for Presidential electors was sharply called to the attention of the people more than four years ago.

It is to be hoped that some well-defined measure may be devised before another national election, which will render unnecessary a resort to any expedient of a temporary character, for the determination of questions upon contested returns.

Questions which concern the very existence of the Government and the liberties of the people were suggested by the prolonged illness of the late President, and his consequent incapacity to perform the functions of his office.

It is provided by the second article of the Constitution, in the fifth clause of its first section, that "in case of the removal of the President from office, or of his death, resignation, or inability to discharge the powers and duties of said office, the same shall devolve on the Vice-President."

What is the intendment of the Constitution in its specification of "inability to discharge the powers and duties of said office," as one of the contingencies which calls the Vice-President to the exercise of Presidential functions?

Is the inability limited in its nature to long-continued intellectual incapacity, or has it a broader import?

What must be its extent and duration?

How must its existence be established?

Has the President, whose inability is the subject of inquiry, any voice in determining whether or not it exists, or is the decision of that momentous and delicate question confided to the Vice-President, or is it contemplated by the Constitution that Congress should provide by law precisely what should constitute inability, and how and by what tribunal or authority it should be ascertained?

If the inability proves to be temporary in its nature, and during its continuance the Vice-President lawfully exercises the functions of the Executive, by what tenure does he hold his office?

Does he continue as President for the remainder of the four years' term?

Or would the elected President, if his inability should cease in the interval, be empowered to resume his office?

And if having such lawful authority he should exercise it, would the Vice-President be thereupon empowered to resume his powers and duties as such?

I cannot doubt that these important questions will receive your early and thoughtful consideration.

Deeply impressed with the gravity of the responsibilities which have so unexpectedly devolved upon me, it will be my constant purpose to co-operate with you in such measures as will promote the glory of the country and the prosperity of its people.

CHESTER A. ARTHUR.

WASHINGTON, *December* 6, 1881.

MESSAGE.

USE OF UNITED STATES TROOPS IN NEBRASKA.

MARCH 18, 1882.

MESSAGE

BILL ENTITLED "AN ACT TO EXECUTE CERTAIN TREATY STIPULATIONS RELATING TO CHINESE," WITH OBJECTIONS THERETO,

APRIL 4, 1882.

73

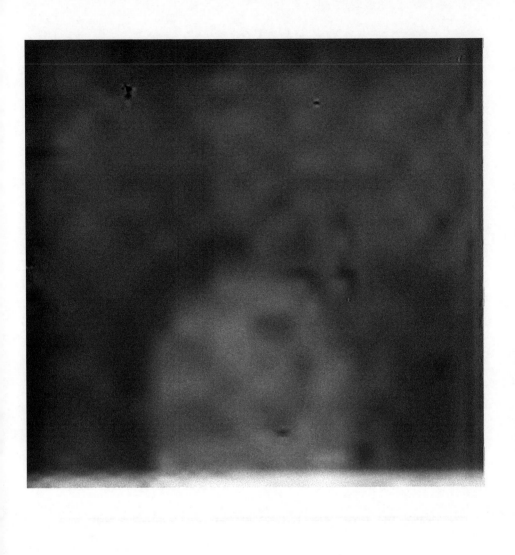

MESSAGE.

After careful consideration of Senate bill No. 71, entitled "An act to execute certain treaty stipulations relating to Chinese," I herewith return it to the Senate, in which it originated, with my objections to its passage.

A nation is justified in repudiating its treaty obligations only when they are in conflict with great paramount interests. Even then all possible reasonable means for modifying or changing those obligations by mutual agreement should be exhausted before resorting to the supreme right of refusal to comply with them.

These rules have governed the United States in their past intercourse with other powers as one of the family of nations. I am persuaded that if Congress can feel that this act violates the faith of the nation, as pledged to China, it will concur with me in rejecting this particular mode of regulating Chinese immigration, and will endeavor to find another which shall meet the expectations of the people of the United States without coming in conflict with the rights of China.

The present treaty relations between that power and the United States spring from an antagonism which arose between our paramount domestic interests and our previous relations.

The treaty commonly known as the Burlingame Treaty conferred upon Chinese subjects the right of voluntary emigration to the United States for the purposes of curiosity or trade, or as permanent residents, and was in all respects reciprocal as to citizens of the United States in China. It gave to the voluntary emigrant coming to the United States the right to travel there or to reside there, with all the privileges, immunities, or exemptions enjoyed by the citizens or subjects of the most favored nation.

75

Under the operation of this treaty it was found that the institutions of the United States and the character of its people and their means of obtaining a livelihood might be seriously affected by the unrestricted introduction of Chinese labor. Congress attempted to alleviate this condition by legislation, but the act which it passed proved to be in violation of our treaty obligations, and, being returned by the President with his objections, failed to become a law.

Diplomatic relief was then sought. A new treaty was concluded with China. Without abrogating the Burlingame treaty, it was agreed to modify it so far that the Government of the United States might regulate, limit, or suspend the coming of Chinese laborers to the United States, or their residence therein; but that it should not absolutely prohibit them, and that the limitation or suspension should be reasonable, and should apply only to Chinese who might go to the United States as laborers, other classes not being included in the limitations. This treaty is unilateral, not reciprocal. It is a concession from China to the United States, in limitation of the rights which she was enjoying under the Burlingame treaty. It leaves us by our own act to determine when and how we will enforce those limitations. China may therefore fairly have a right to expect that in enforcing them we will take good care not to overstep the grant and take more than has been conceded to us.

It is but a year since this new treaty, under the operation of the Constitution, became part of the supreme law of the land; and the present act is the first attempt to exercise the more enlarged powers which it relinquishes to the United States.

In its first article the United States is empowered to decide whether the coming of Chinese laborers to the United States, or their residence therein, affects or threatens to affect our interests, or to endanger good order, either within the whole country or in any part of it. The act recites that "in the opinion of the Government of the United States the coming of Chinese laborers to this country endangers the good order of certain localities thereof." But the act itself is much broader than the recital. It acts upon residence as well as immigration, and its provisions are effective throughout the United States. I think it may fairly be accepted as an expression of the opinion of Congress that the coming of such laborers to the

United States, or their residence here, affects our interests, and endangers good order throughout the country. On this point I should feel it my duty to accept the views of Congress.

The first article further conveys the power upon this Government to regulate, limit, or suspend, but not actually to prohibit, the coming of such laborers to, or their residence in, the United States. The negotiators of the treaty have recorded with unusual fullness their understanding of the sense and meaning with which these words were used.

As to the class of persons to be affected by the treaty, the Americans inserted in their draft a provision that the words "Chinese laborers" signify all immigration other than that for "teaching, trade, travel, study, and curiosity." The Chinese objected to this that it operated to include artizans in the class of laborers whose immigration might be forbidden. The Americans replied that they "could" not consent that artizans shall be excluded from the class of Chinese laborers, for it is this very competition of skilled labor, in the cities where the Chinese labor immigration concentrates, which has caused the embarrassment and popular discontent. In the subsequent negotiations this definition dropped out, and does not appear in the treaty. Article II of the treaty confers the rights, privileges, immunities, and exemptions which are accorded to citizens and subjects of the most favored nation upon Chinese subjects proceeding to the United States as teachers, students, merchants, or from curiosity. The American commissioners report that the Chinese Government claimed that in this article they did, by exclusion, provide that nobody should be entitled to claim the benefit of the general provisions of the Burlingame treaty but those who might go to the United States in those capacities, or for those purposes. I accept this as the definition of the word "laborers," as used in the treaty.

As to the power of legislating respecting this class of persons, the new treaty provides that we "may not absolutely prohibit" their coming or their residence. The Chinese commissioners gave notice in the outset that they would never agree to a prohibition of voluntary emigration. Notwithstanding this the United States commissioners submitted a draft in which it was provided that the United States might "regulate, limit, suspend, or prohibit" it. The

• Chinese refused to accept this. The Americans replied that they were "willing to consult the wishes of the Chinese Government in preserving the principle of free intercourse between the people of the two countries, as established by existing treaties, provided that the right of the United States Government to use its discretion in guarding against any possible evils of immigration of Chinese laborers is distinctly recognized. Therefore, if such concession removes all difficulty on the part of the Chinese commissioners (but only in that case), the United States commissioners will agree to remove the word "prohibit" from their article, and to use the words "regulate, limit, or suspend." The Chinese reply to this can only be inferred from the fact that in the place of an agreement, as proposed by our commissioners, that we might prohibit the coming or residence of Chinese laborers, there was inserted in the treaty an agreement that we might not do it.

The remaining words "regulate, limit, and suspend," first appear in the American draft. When it was submitted to the Chinese they said, "We infer that of the phrases regulate, limit, suspend, or prohibit, the first is a general expression referring to the others." "We are entirely ready to negotiate with your Excellencies to the end that a limitation either in point of time or of numbers may be fixed upon the emigration of Chinese laborers to the United States." At a subsequent interview they said, that "by limitation in number they meant, for example, that the United States having, as they supposed, a record of the number of immigrants in each year, as well as the total number of Chinese now there, that no more should be allowed to go in any one year in future than either the greatest number which had gone in any year in the past, or that the total number should never be allowed to exceed the number now there. As to limitation of time they meant, for example, that Chinese should be allowed to go in alternate years, or every third year, or, for example, that they should not be allowed to go for two, three, or five years." At a subsequent conference the Americans said, "The Chinese commissioners have in their project explicitly recognized the right of the United States to use some discretion, and have proposed a limitation as to time and number. This *is* the right to regulate, limit, or suspend."

In one of the conferences the Chinese asked the Americans whether they could give them any idea of the laws which would be passed to carry the powers into execution. The Americans answered that this could hardly be done, "that the United States Government might never deem it necessary to exercise this power. It would depend upon circumstances. If Chinese immigration concentrated in cities where it threatened public order, or if it confined itself to localities where it was an injury to the interests of the American people, the Government of the United States would undoubtedly take steps to prevent such accumulations of Chinese. If, on the contrary, there was no large immigration, or if there were sections of the country where such immigration was clearly beneficial, then the legislation of the United States, under this power, would be adapted to such circumstances. For example, there might be a demand for Chinese labor in the South, and a surplus of such labor in California, and Congress might legislate in accordance with these facts. In general, the legislation would be in view of, and depend upon the circumstances of the situation at the moment such legislation became necessary." The Chinese commissioners said this explanation was satisfactory; that they had not intended to ask for a draft of any special act, but for some general idea how the power would be exercised. What had just been said gave them the explanation which they wanted.

With this entire accord as to the meaning of the words they were about to employ, and the object of the legislation which might be had in consequence, the parties signed the treaty, in Article I of which "the Government of China agrees that the Government of the United States may regulate, limit, or suspend such coming or residence, but may not absolutely prohibit it. The limitation or suspension shall be reasonable, and shall apply only to Chinese who may go to the United States as laborers, other classes not being included in the limitations. Legislation taken in regard to Chinese laborers will be of such a character only as is necessary to enforce the regulation limitation or suspension of immigration."

The first section of the act provides that "from and after the expiration of sixty days next after the passage of this act, and until the expiration of twenty years next after the passage of this act, the coming of Chinese laborers be, and the same is hereby, suspended, and during such suspension it shall not be lawful for any Chinese laborer to come, or having so come after the expiration of said sixty days, to remain within the United States."

The examination which I have made of the treaty, and of the declarations which its negotiators have left on record of the meaning of its language, leaves no doubt in my mind that neither contracting party in concluding the treaty of 1880 contemplated the passage of an act prohibiting immigration for twenty years, which is nearly a generation, or thought that such a period would be a reasonable suspension or limitation, or intended to change the provisions of the Burlingame treaty to that extent. I regard this provision of the act as a breach of our national faith; and being unable to bring myself in harmony with the views of Congress on this vital point, the honor of the country constrains me to return the act with this objection to its passage.

Deeply convinced of the necessity of some legislation on this subject, and concurring fully with Congress in many of the objects which are sought to be accomplished, I avail myself of the opportunity to point out some other features of the present act which, in my opinion, can be modified to advantage.

The classes of Chinese who still enjoy the protection of the Burlingame treaty are entitled to the privileges, immunities, and exemptions accorded to citizens and subjects of the most favored nation. We have treaties with many powers which permit their citizens and subjects to reside within the United States and carry on business under the same laws and regulations which are enforced against citizens of the United States. I think it may be doubted whether provisions requiring personal registration and the taking out of passports which are not imposed upon natives can be required of Chinese. Without expressing an opinion on that point, I may invite the attention of Congress to the fact that the system of personal registration and passports is undemocratic and hostile to the spirit of our institutions. I doubt the wisdom of putting an entering wedge of this kind into our laws. A nation like the United States, jealous of the liberties of its citizens, may well hesitate before it incorporates into its polity a system which is fast disappearing in Europe before the progress of liberal institutions. A wide experience has shown how futile such precautions are, and how easily passports may be borrowed, exchanged, or even forged by persons interested to do so.

If it is nevertheless thought that a passport is the most convenient way for identifying the Chinese entitled to the protection of the Burlingame treaty, it may still be doubted whether they ought to be required to register. It is certainly our duty under the Burlingame treaty to make their stay in the United States, in the operation of general laws upon them, as nearly like that of our own citizens as we can consistently with our right to shut out the laborers. No good purpose is served in requiring them to register.

My attention has been called by the Chinese minister to the fact that the bill as it stands makes no provision for the transit across the United States of Chinese subjects now residing in foreign countries. I think that this point may well claim the attention of Congress in legislating on this subject.

I have said that good faith requires us to suspend the immigration of Chinese laborers for a less period than twenty years; I now add that good policy points in the same direction.

Our intercourse with China is of recent date. Our first treaty with that power is not yet forty years old. It is only since we acquired California and established a great seat of commerce on the Pacific that we may be said to have broken down the barriers which fenced in that ancient monarchy. The Burlingame treaty naturally followed. Under the spirit which inspired it, many thousand Chinese laborers came to the United States. No one can say that the country has not profited by their work. They were largely instrumental in constructing the railways which connect the Atlantic with the Pacific. The States of the Pacific slope are full of evidences of their industry. Enterprises profitable alike to the capitalist and to the laborer of Caucasian origin would have lain dormant but for them. A time has now come when it is supposed that they are not needed, and when it is thought by Congress and by those most acquainted with the subject that it is best to try to get along without them. There may, however, be other sections of the country where this species of labor may be advantageously employed without inter-

6*

fering with the laborers of our own race. In making the proposed
experiment, it may be the part of wisdom as well as of good faith to
fix the length of the experimental period with reference to this fact.

Experience has shown that the trade of the East is the key to
national wealth and influence. The opening of China to the commerce of the whole world has benefited no section of it more than
the States of our own Pacific slope. The State of California, and
its great maritime port especially, have reaped enormous advantages
from this source. Blessed with an exceptional climate, enjoying an
unrivaled harbor, with the riches of a great agricultural and mining
State in its rear, and the wealth of the whole Union pouring into it
over its lines of railway, San Francisco has before it an incalculable
future, if our friendly and amicable relations with Asia remain undisturbed. It needs no argument to show that the policy which we
now propose to adopt must have a direct tendency to repel Oriental
nations from us, and to drive their trade and commerce into more
friendly lands. It may be that the great and paramount interest of
protecting our labor from Asiatic competition may justify us in a
permanent adoption of this policy. But it is wiser, in the first place,
to make a shorter experiment, with a view hereafter of maintaining
permanently only such features as time and experience may commend.

I transmit herewith copies of the papers relating to the recent
treaty with China, which accompanied the confidential message of
President Hayes to the Senate of the 10th January, 1881, and also
a copy of a memorandum respecting the act herewith returned, which
was handed to the Secretary of State by the Chinese minister in
Washington.

                                    CHESTER A. ARTHUR.

EXECUTIVE MANSION,
    Washington, April 4, 1882.

MESSAGE.

—

MISSISSIPPI RIVER COMMISSION.

APRIL 17, 1882.

MESSAGE.

To the Senate and House of Representatives:

I transmit herewith a letter, dated the 29th ultimo, from the Secretary of War, inclosing copy of a communication from the Mississippi River Commission, in which the Commission recommends that an appropriation may be made of $1,010,000 for "closing existing gaps in levees," in addition to the like sum for which an estimate has already been submitted.

The subject is one of such importance that I deem it proper to recommend early and favorable consideration of the recommendations of the Commission.   Having possession of and jurisdiction over the river, Congress, with a view of improving its navigation and protecting the people of the valley from floods, has for years caused surveys of the river to be made, for the purpose of acquiring knowledge of the laws that control it and of its phenomena.   By act approved June 28, 1879, the Mississippi River Commission was created, composed of able engineers.   Section 4 of the act provides that "it shall be the duty of said Commission to take into consideration and mature such plan or plans and estimates as will correct permanently, locate and deepen the channel, and protect the banks of the Mississippi River; improve and give safety and ease to the navigation thereof; prevent destructive floods; promote and facilitate commerce, trade, and the postal service."

The constitutionality of a law making appropriations in aid of these objects cannot be questioned.   While the report of the Commission submitted and the plans proposed for the river's improvement seem justified as well on scientific principles as by experience and the approval of the people most interested, I desire to leave it to the judgment of Congress to decide upon the best plan for the permanent and complete improvement of the navigation of the river, and for the protection of the valley.

The immense losses and widespread suffering of the people dwelling near the river induce me to urge upon Congress the propriety of not only making an appropriation to close the gaps in the levees occasioned by the recent floods, as recommended by the Commission, but that Congress should inaugurate measures for the permanent improvement of the navigation of the river and security of the valley. It may be that such a system of improvement would as it progressed require the appropriation of twenty or thirty millions of dollars; even such an expenditure, extending as it must over several years, cannot be regarded as extravagant in view of the immense interest involved. The safe and convenient navigation of the Mississippi is a matter of concern to all sections of the country; but to the Northwest with its immense harvests needing chief transportation to the sea, and to the inhabitants of the river valley whose lives and property depend upon the proper construction of the safeguards which protect them from the floods, it is of vital importance that a well-matured and comprehensive plan for improvement should be put into operation with as little delay as possible. , The cotton product of the region subject to the devastating floods is a source of wealth to the nation and of great importance in keeping the balances of trade in our favor.

It may not be inopportune to mention that this Government has imposed and collected some seventy millions of dollars by a tax on cotton, in the production of which the population of the Lower Mississippi is largely engaged, and it does not seem inequitable to return a portion of this tax to those who contributed it, particularly as such an action will also result in an important gain to the country at large, and especially so to the great and rich States of the Northwest and the Mississippi Valley.

CHESTER A. ARTHUR.

EXECUTIVE MANSION, *April 17, 1882.*

MESSAGE

CONCERNING THE

BOUNDARY BETWEEN THE UNITED STATES AND MEXICO,

APRIL 18, 1882.

H7

MESSAGE.

I transmit herewith, for the consideration of Congress, a note addressed by the minister plenipotentiary of Mexico to the Secretary of State, proposing the conclusion of a convention between the two countries for defining the boundary between the United States and Mexico from the Rio Grande westward to the Pacific Ocean, by the erection of durable monuments. I also lay before Congress a letter on the same subject with its accompaniment, from the Secretary of War, to whom the proposition was referred by the Secretary of State for the expression of his views thereon.

I deem it important that the boundary line between the two countries, as defined by existing treaties and already once surveyed, should be run anew and defined by suitable permanent monuments. By so doing uncertainty will be prevented as to jurisdiction in criminal and municipal affairs, and questions be averted which may at any time in the near future arise with the growth of population on the border.

Moreover, I conceive that the willing and speedy assent of the Government of the United States to the proposal thus to determine the existing stipulated boundary with permanence and precision will be in some sense an assurance to Mexico that the unauthorized suspicion which of late years seems to have gained some credence in that republic that the United States covets and seeks to annex neighboring territory is without foundation. That which the United States seeks, and which the definite settlement of the boundary in the proposed manner will promote, is a confiding and friendly feeling between the two nations, leading to advantageous commerce and closer commercial relations.

I have to suggest that, in accepting this proposal, suitable provision be made for an adequate military force on the frontier to protect the surveying parties from hostile Indians. The troops so employed will, at the same time, protect the settlers on the border and help to prevent marauding on both sides by the nomadic Indians.

CHESTER A. ARTHUR.

EXECUTIVE MANSION,
     Washington, April 18, 1882.

MESSAGE.

AMERICAN PEACE CONGRESS.

APRIL 18, 1882.

MESSAGE.

To the Senate and House of Representatives:

I send herewith a copy of the circular invitation extended to all the independent countries of North and South America to participate in a general congress, to be held in the city of Washington on the 22d of November next, for the purpose of considering and discussing the methods of preventing war between the nations of America.

In giving this invitation I was not unaware that there existed differences between several of the republics of South America which would militate against the happy results which might otherwise be expected from such an assemblage. The differences indicated are such as exist between Chili and Peru, between Mexico and Guatemala, and between the States of Central America.

It was hoped that these differences would disappear before the time fixed for the meeting of the congress. This hope has not been realized.

Having observed that the authority of the President to convene such a congress has been questioned, I beg leave to state that the Constitution confers upon the President the power, by and with the advice and consent of the Senate, to make treaties, and that this provision confers the power to take all requisite measures to initiate them, and to this end the President may freely confer with one or several commissioners or delegates from other nations. The congress contemplated by the invitation could only effect any valuable result by its conclusions eventually taking the form of a treaty of peace between the States represented; and, besides, the invitation to the States of North and South America is merely a preliminary act of which constitutionality or the want of it can hardly be affirmed.

It has been suggested that while the International Congress would

93

have no power to affect the rights of nationalities there represented, still Congress might be unwilling to subject the existing treaty rights of the United States on the Isthmus and elsewhere on the continent to be clouded and rendered uncertain by the expression of the opinions of a congress composed largely of interested parties.

I am glad to have it in my power to refer to the Congress of the United States, as I now do, the propriety of convening the suggested International Congress, that I may thus be informed of its views, which it will be my pleasure to carry out. Inquiry having been made by some of the republics invited whether it is intended that this International Congress shall convene, it is important that Congress should, at as early a day as is convenient, inform me, by resolution or otherwise, of its opinion in the premises. My action will be in harmony with such expression.

CHESTER A. ARTHUR.

EXECUTIVE MANSION,
     Washington, April 18, 1882.

MESSAGE

DISORDERS AND LAWLESSNESS IN ARIZONA.

APRIL 26, 1882.

95

MESSAGE.

To the Senate and House of Representatives:

By recent information, received from official and other sources, I am advised that an alarming state of disorder continues to exist within the Territory of Arizona, and that lawlessness has already gained such head there as to require a resort to extraordinary means to repress it.

The governor of the Territory, under date of the 31st ultimo, reports that violence and anarchy prevail, particularly in Cochise County, and along the Mexican border; that robbery, murder, and resistance to law have become so common as to cease causing surprise; and that the people are greatly intimidated and losing confidence in the protection of the law. I transmit his communication herewith, and call especial attention thereto.

In a telegram from the General of the Army, dated at Tucson, Arizona, on the 11th instant, herewith transmitted, that officer states that he hears of lawlessness and disorders, which seem well attested, and that the civil officers have not sufficient force to make arrests and hold the prisoners for trial, or punish them when convicted.

Much of this disorder is caused by armed bands of desperadoes known as cowboys, by whom depredations are not only committed within the Territory, but it is alleged predatory incursions made therefrom into Mexico. In my message to Congress at the beginning of the present session, I called attention to the existence of these bands, and suggested that the setting on foot, within our own Territory, of brigandage and armed marauding expeditions against friendly nations and their citizens be made punishable as an offense against the United States. I renew this suggestion.

To effectually repress the lawlessness prevailing within the Territory, a prompt execution of the process of the courts and vigorous

7*

enforcement of the laws against offenders are needed.   This the civil authorities there are unable to do, without the aid of other means and forces than they can now avail themselves of.

To meet the present exigencies, the governor asks that provision be made by Congress to enable him to employ and maintain, temporarily, a volunteer militia force, to aid the civil authorities, the members of which force to be invested with the same powers and authority as are conferred by the laws of the Territory upon peace officers thereof.

On the ground of economy, as well as effectiveness, however, it appears to me to be more advisable to permit the co-operation with the civil authorities of a part of the Army as a *posse comitatus*.

Believing that this, in addition to such use of the Army as may be made under the powers already conferred by section 5298, Revised Statutes, would be adequate to secure the accomplishment of the ends in view, I again call the attention of Congress to the expediency of so amending section 15 of the act of June 18, 1878, chapter 263, as to allow the military forces to be employed as a *posse comitatus* to assist the civil authorities within a Territory to execute the laws therein.   This use of the Army, as I have in my former message observed, would not seem to be within the alleged evil against which that legislation was aimed.

CHESTER A. ARTHUR.

EXECUTIVE MANSION, *April 26, 1882.*

PROCLAMATION

CONCERNING

LAWLESSNESS IN ARIZONA.

MAY 3, 1882.

PROCLAMATION.

A PROCLAMATION.

Whereas it is provided in the laws of the United States that "whenever, by reason of unlawful obstructions, combinations, or assemblages of persons, or rebellion against the authority of the Government of the United States, it shall become impracticable, in the judgment of the President, to enforce, by the ordinary course of judicial proceedings, the laws of the United States within any State or Territory, it shall be lawful for the President to call forth the militia of any or all the States, and to employ such parts of the land and naval forces of the United States as he may deem necessary to enforce the faithful execution of the laws of the United States, or to suppress such rebellion, in whatever State or Territory thereof the laws of the United States may be forcibly opposed, or the execution thereof forcibly obstructed";

And whereas it has been made to appear satisfactorily to me, by information received from the governor of the Territory of Arizona, and from the General of the Army of the United States, and other reliable sources, that in consequence of unlawful combinations of evil-disposed persons who are banded together to oppose and obstruct the execution of the laws, it has become impracticable to enforce, by the ordinary course of judicial proceedings, the laws of the United States within that Territory, and that the laws of the United States have been therein forcibly opposed and the execution thereof forcibly resisted;

And whereas the laws of the United States require that whenever it may be necessary, in the judgment of the President, to use the military forces for the purpose of enforcing the faithful execution of the laws of the United States, he shall forthwith, by proclamation, command such insurgents to disperse and retire peaceably to their respective abodes, within a limited time:

Now, therefore, I, CHESTER A. ARTHUR, President of the United States, do hereby admonish all good citizens of the United States, and especially of the Territory of Arizona, against aiding, countenancing, abetting, or taking part in any such unlawful proceedings, and I do hereby warn all persons engaged in or connected with said obstruction of the laws, to disperse and retire peaceably to their respective abodes on or before noon of the fifteenth day of May.

In witness whereof I have hereunto set my hand and caused the seal of the United States to be affixed.

Done at the city of Washington this third day of May, in the year of our Lord eighteen hundred and eighty-two, and of the Independence of the United States the one hundred and sixth.

[SEAL.] 　　　　　　　　　　　CHESTER A. ARTHUR.

By the President:

FRED'K T. FRELINGHUYSEN,
Secretary of State.

MESSAGE.

___

CARRIAGE OF PASSENGERS BY SEA.

JULY 1, 1882.

MESSAGE.

Herewith I return House bill No. 2744, entitled "An act to regulate the carriage of passengers by sea," without my approval. In doing this, I regret that I am not able to give my assent to an act which has received the sanction of the majority of both houses of Congress.

The object proposed to be secured by the act is meritorious and philanthropic. Some correct and accurate legislation upon this subject is undoubtedly necessary. Steamships that bring large bodies of emigrants must be subjected to strict legal enactments, so as to prevent the passengers from being exposed to hardship and suffering; and such legislation should be made as will give them abundance of space and air and light, protecting their health by affording all reasonable comforts and conveniences, and by providing for the quantity and quality of the food to be furnished, and all of the other essentials of roomy, safe, and healthful accommodations in their passage across the sea.

A statute providing for all this is absolutely needed, and in the spirit of humane legislation must be enacted. The present act by most of its provisions will obtain and secure this protection for such passengers, and were it not for some serious errors contained in it, would be most willingly approved by me.

My objections are these: In the first section, in lines from 13 to 24 inclusive, it is provided "that the compartments or spaces," &c., "shall be of sufficient dimensions to allow for each and any passenger," &c., "a hundred cubic feet, if the compartment or space is located on the first deck next below the *uppermost deck* of the vessel," &c., "or one hundred and twenty cubic feet for each passenger,"

&c., "if the compartment or space is located on the second deck below the *uppermost deck* of the vessel," &c.   "It shall not be lawful to carry or bring passengers on any deck other than the two decks mentioned," &c.

Nearly all of the new, and most of the improved ocean steamers, have a spar-deck, which is above the main deck.   The main deck was, in the old style of steamers, the only uppermost deck.   The spar-deck is a comparatively new feature of the large and costly steamships, and is now practically the uppermost deck; below this spar-deck is the main deck.   Because of the misuse of the words "uppermost deck" instead of the use of the words "main deck," by this act, the result will be to exclude nearly all of the large steamships from carrying passengers anywhere but on the main deck and on the deck below, which is the steerage-deck, and to leave the orlop, or lower deck, heretofore used for passengers, useless and unoccupied by passengers.   This objection, which is now presented in connection with others that will be presently explained, will, if this act is enforced as it is now phrased, render useless for passenger traffic and expose to heavy loss all of the great ocean steam lines; and it will also hinder emigration, as there will not be ships enough that could accept these conditions to carry all who may now wish to come.

The use of the new and the hitherto unknown term "uppermost deck" creates this difficulty, and I cannot consent to have an abuse of terms like this to operate thus injuriously to these large fleets of ships.   The passengers will not be benefited by such a statute, but emigration will be hindered, if not for a while almost prevented, for many.

Again, the act in the first section, from line 31 to line 35 inclusive, provides: "And such passengers shall not be carried or brought in any between-decks, nor in any compartment," &c., "the clear height of which is less than seven feet."   Between the decks of all ships are the beams; they are about a foot in width.   The legal method of ascertaining tonnage for the purpose of taxation is to measure between the beams from the floor to the ceiling.   If this becomes a law, the space required would be 8 feet from floor to ceiling; and this is impracticable, for in all ships the spaces between decks are adjusted in proportion to the dimensions of the ship; and if these spaces between decks are changed so as not to correspond in their proportions with the dimensions of the vessel the ship will not work well in the sea, her sailing qualities will be injured, and she will be rendered unfit for service.

It is only in great ships of vast tonnage that the height between decks can be increased. All the ordinary-sized ships are necessarily constructed with 7 feet space in the interval between the beams from the floor to the ceiling. To adopt this act, with this provision, would be to drive out of the service of transporting passengers most of all the steamships now in such trade, and no practical good obtained by it, for really, with the exception of the narrow beam, the space between the decks is now 7 feet. The purpose of the space commanded by the act is to obtain sufficient air and ventilation, and that is actually now given to the passenger by the 7 feet that exists in all of these vessels between floor and ceiling.

There is also another objection that I must suggest. In section 12, from line 14 to line 24, it is provided: "Before such vessel shall be cleared or may lawfully depart, &c., the master of said vessel shall furnish, &c., a correct list of all passengers who have been or are intended to be taken on board the vessel, and shall specify," &c. This provision would prevent the clearing of the vessel. Steam vessels start at an appointed hour, and with punctuality. Down almost to the very hour of their departure new passengers, other than those who have engaged their passage, constantly come on board. If this provision is to be the law they must be rejected, for the ship cannot, without incurring heavy penalties, take passengers whose names are not set forth on the list required before such vessel shall be cleared. They should be allowed to take such new passengers upon condition that they would furnish an additional list containing such persons' names. There are other points of objection of a minor character that might be presented for consideration if the bill could be reconsidered and amended, but the three that I have recited are conspicuous defects in a bill that ought to be a code for such a purpose, clear and explicit, free from all such objections. The practical result of this law would be to subject all of the competing lines of large ocean steamers to great losses. By restricting their carrying accommodations it would also stay the current of emigration that it is our policy to encourage as well as to protect. A good bill, correctly phrased, and expressing and naming in plain, well-known technical terms the proper and usual places and decks, where passengers are and ought to be placed and carried, will receive my prompt and immediate assent as a public necessity and blessing.

CHESTER A. ARTHUR.

EXECUTIVE MANSION, *July 1, 1882.*

MESSAGE

TRANSMITTING

THE CLAIMS OF BENJAMIN WEIL AND LA ABRA SILVER MINING COMPANY AGAINST MEXICO

JULY 20, 1882.

MESSAGE.

I transmit herewith to the Senate for its consideration, with a view to ratification, a convention between the United States and Mexico, providing for the reopening and retrying of the claims of Benjamin Weil and La Abra Silver Mining Company against Mexico, which was signed on the 13th instant.

A report of the Secretary of State with its accompanying correspondence, transmitted to the Senate this day in response to the resolution of December 21, 1881, will show the antecedents of the negotiation which resulted in the accompanying convention. In view of the accumulation of testimony presented by Mexico relative to these two claims, I have deemed it proper to avail myself of the authority given to the Executive by the Constitution, and of which authority the act of Congress of June 18, 1878, is declarative, to effect a rehearing of these cases. I therefore empowered the Secretary of State to negotiate with the minister of Mexico a convention to that end.

The more important correspondence preliminary to the treaty is herewith transmitted.

It will be seen by the stipulations of the treaty that the rehearing will have no retroactive effect as to payments already distributed, that the *bona fide* interests of third parties are simply secured, and that the Government of the United States is fully guarded against any liability resulting from the rehearing.

CHESTER A. ARTHUR.

Executive Mansion, *July 20, 1882.*

MESSAGE.

APPROPRIATIONS FOR RIVERS AND HARBORS.

AUGUST 1, 1882.

MESSAGE.

TO THE HOUSE OF REPRESENTATIVES:

Having watched with much interest the progress of House bill No. 6242, entitled "An act making appropriations for the construction, repair, and preservation of certain works on rivers and harbors, and for other purposes," and having, since it was received, carefully examined it, after mature consideration I am constrained to return it herewith to the House of Representatives, in which it originated, without my signature, and with my objections to its passage.

Many of the appropriations in the bill are clearly for the general welfare, and most beneficent in their character. Two of the objects for which provision is made were by me considered so important that I felt it my duty to direct to them the attention of Congress. In my annual message in December last I urged the vital importance of legislation for the reclamation of the marshes and for the establishment of the harbor lines along the Potomac front. In April last, by special message, I recommended an appropriation for the improvement of the Mississippi River. It is not necessary that I say that, when my signature would make the bill appropriating for these and other valuable national objects a law, it is with great reluctance and only under a sense of duty that I withhold it.

My principal objection to the bill is that it contains appropriations for purposes not for the common defense or general welfare, and which do not promote commerce among the States. These provisions, on the contrary, are entirely for the benefit of the particular localities in which it is proposed to make the improvements. I regard such appropriation of the public money as beyond the powers given by the Constitution to Congress and the President.

I feel the more bound to withhold my signature from the bill because of the peculiar evils which manifestly result from this infraction of the Constitution.   Appropriations of this nature, to be devoted purely to local objects, tend to an increase in number and in amount.   As the citizens of one State find that money, to raise which they in common with the whole country are taxed, is to be expended for local improvements in another State, they demand similar benefits for themselves; and it is not unnatural that they should seek to indemnify themselves for such use of the public funds by securing appropriations for similar improvements in their own neighborhood.   Thus as the bill becomes more objectionable it secures more support.   This result is invariable, and necessarily follows a neglect to observe the constitutional limitations imposed upon the law-making power.

The appropriations for river and harbor improvements have, under the influences to which I have alluded, increased year by year, out of proportion to the progress of the country, great as that has been. In 1870 the aggregate appropriation was $3,975,900; in 1875, $6,648,517.50; in 1880, $8,976,500; and in 1881, $11,451,300; while by the present act there is appropriated $18,743,875.

While feeling every disposition to leave to the Legislature the responsibility of determining what amount should be appropriated for the purposes of the bill—so long as the appropriations are con- fined to objects indicated by the grant of power—I cannot escape the conclusion that, as a part of the law-making power of the Govern- ment, the duty devolves upon me to withhold my signature from a bill containing appropriations which, in my opinion, greatly exceed in amount the needs of the country for the present fiscal year.   It being the usage to provide money for these purposes by annual ap- propriation bills, the President is in effect directed to expend so large an amount of money within so brief a period that the expendi- ture cannot be made economically and advantageously.

The extravagant expenditure of public money is an evil not to be measured by the value of that money to the people who are taxed for it.   They sustain a greater injury in the demoralizing effect pro- duced upon those who are intrusted with official duty through all the ramifications of Government.

These objections could be removed and every constitutional pur- pose readily attained should Congress enact that one-half only of the aggregate amount provided for in the bill be appropriated for expenditure during the fiscal year, and that the sum so appropriated be expended only for such objects named in the bill as the Secretary of War under the direction of the President shall determine; provided that in no case shall the expenditure for any one purpose exceed the sum now designated by the bill for that purpose.

I feel authorized to make this suggestion because of the duty imposed upon the President by the Constitution "to recommend to the consideration of Congress such measures as he shall judge necessary and expedient," and because it is my earnest desire that the public works which are in progress shall suffer no injury. Congress will also convene again in four months, when this whole subject will be open for their consideration.

CHESTER A. ARTHUR.

EXECUTIVE MANSION, *August 1, 1882.*

ADDRESS

BOSTON, OCTOBER 11, 1882.

ADDRESS.

I can scarcely trust myself to utter in this historic hall, whose walls have so oft resounded with the eloquence of orators and statesmen, the words by which I must attest my gratitude for your cordial and enthusiastic welcome.

If I looked within myself to find its cause, I should indeed be oppressed by a sense of my own undeserving. But I well know that the flattering demonstrations with which this day has been crowded are attributable in but small measure to the prompting of personal regard. They but serve to give voice to the unstinted loyalty of Boston and Massachusetts to the Government of the United States. They betoken the respect which is entertained by the people of this grand old Commonwealth and of this magnificent city for the Federal authority which they themselves have aided to constitute. It is in this spirit that I accept and thank you for your gracious greetings.

ADDRESS

COMMENDING

THE PURPOSES OF THE WEBSTER HISTORICAL SOCIETY,

MARSHFIELD, OCTOBER 13, 1882.

ADDRESS.

Mr. Chairman and Gentlemen:

It is fortunately in accord with the proprieties of this occasion, no less than my own inclination, that I should confine within narrow limits my acknowledgment of your flattering salutation. I am deeply moved by the warmth of your greeting; it is but a fresh display of that splendid hospitality which since I came within the borders of Massachusetts has everywhere obstructed my way with demonstrations of courtesy and respect.

I trust that neither my gratitude nor my sympathy with the purposes which have turned our reverent footsteps hitherward to-day will be measured by my poor endeavor to give them expression. The character and genius of that illustrious man whose life moved grandly among so many fields of eminence, in commemoration of whose birth a hundred years ago we have gathered to-day amid the beautiful scenes where he found rest from the fret and worry of life, have for more than a generation been the theme of discussion and eulogy.

I shall not attempt to labor in the field over which so many flashing sickles have swept and which has so long been crowded with illustrious gleaners. But I may perhaps be permitted to declare my approval of what has been accomplished by this society for the object for which it is founded. It is asserted upon what I suppose to be trustworthy authority that Mr. Webster expressed the wish near the close of his life that for aiding to transmit his fame to future generations of his countrymen, for kindling in their hearts the flames of patriotism, for arousing their devotion to the principles of constitutional government, there should be disseminated far and wide among them such recorded efforts of his genius as seemed most worthy to be thus preserved. Many of the loftiest and most

125

inspiring of Mr. Webster's utterances have long been as familiar as
household words in the mouth of every school-boy in the land, but
it is doubtless true that many others, scarcely less dignified in spirit,
masterly in reasoning, and splendid in diction, are comparatively
unknown.

In all that you have hitherto done, in all that you may henceforth
do, to secure the result which Mr. Webster wished to bring about
by the collection and circulation of all his works which have permanence—and which of them has not—I assure you of my earnest
sympathy. Not one of the rising generation of our countrymen
who seeks to be instructed in those political doctrines which are the
basis of our Federal Government, to acquaint himself with the Constitution of his country and the origin, progress, and significance of
its institutions, can by any other course so surely, so speedily attain
that end as by resorting to that great storehouse of eloquence and
wisdom, the published writings of Daniel Webster. And so, gentlemen of the Webster Historical Society, I bid you God-speed in
this and in all other work which you have set yourselves to
accomplish.

Let me once more tender my thanks to you for your hospitality
and express the hope that this noble Commonwealth, its cities, its
villages, its hamlets, and all that dwell within its borders may be
blessed by the abiding presence of prosperity and peace.

PROCLAMATION

APPOINTING

NOVEMBER 30, 1882, AS A DAY OF NATIONAL THANKSGIVING.

OCTOBER 25, 1882.

127

PROCLAMATION.

BY THE PRESIDENT OF THE UNITED STATES OF AMERICA.

A PROCLAMATION.

In conformity with a custom the annual observance of which is justly held in honor by this people, I, CHESTER A. ARTHUR, President of the United States, do hereby set apart Thursday, the thirtieth day of November next, as a day of public thanksgiving.

The blessings demanding our gratitude are numerous and varied. For the peace and amity which subsist between this Republic and all the nations of the world; for the freedom from internal discord and violence; for the increasing friendship between the different sections of the land; for liberty, justice, and constitutional government; for the devotion of the people to our free institutions and their cheerful obedience to mild laws; for the constantly increasing strength of the Republic while extending its privileges to fellow men who come to us; for the improved means of internal communication, and the increased facilities of intercourse with other nations; for the general prevailing health of the year; for the prosperity of all our industries, the liberal return for the mechanic's toil, affording a market for the abundant harvests of the husbandman; for the preservation of the national faith and credit; for wise and generous provision to effect the intellectual and moral education of our youth; for the influence upon the conscience of a restraining and transforming religion; and for the joys of home; for these, and for many other blessings, we should give thanks.

Wherefore, I do recommend that the day above designated be observed throughout the country as a Day of National Thanksgiving and Prayer, and that the people, ceasing from their daily labors and meeting in accordance with their several forms of worship, draw near to the Throne of Almighty God, offering to Him praise and

MESSAGE

TO THE

SENATE AND HOUSE OF REPRESENTATIVES,

DECEMBER 4, 1882.

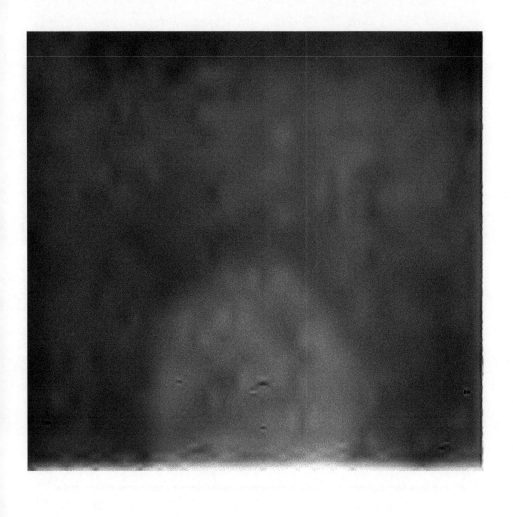

MESSAGE.

It is provided by the Constitution that the President shall from time to time give to the Congress information of the state of the Union, and recommend to their consideration such measures as he shall judge necessary and expedient.

In reviewing the events of the year which has elapsed since the commencement of your sessions, I first call your attention to the gratifying condition of our foreign affairs. Our intercourse with other powers has continued to be of the most friendly character.

Such slight differences as have arisen during the year have been already settled or are likely to reach an early adjustment. The arrest of citizens of the United States in Ireland under recent laws which owe their origin to the disturbed condition of that country has led to a somewhat extended correspondence with the Government of Great Britain. A disposition to respect our rights has been practically manifested by the release of the arrested parties.

The claim of this nation in regard to the supervision and control of any inter-oceanic canal across the American Isthmus has continued to be the subject of conference.

It is likely that time will be more powerful than discussion in removing the divergence between the two nations whose friendship is so closely cemented by the intimacy of their relations and the community of their interests.

Our long-established friendliness with Russia has remained unshaken. It has prompted me to proffer the earnest counsels of this Government that measures be adopted for suppressing the proscription which the Hebrew race in that country has lately suffered. It has not transpired that any American citizen has been subjected to arrest or injury, but our courteous remonstrance has nevertheless been courteously received. There is reason to believe that the time is not far distant when Russia will be able to secure toleration to all faiths within her borders.

At an international convention held at Paris in 1880, and attended by representatives of the United States, an agreement was reached in respect to the protection of trade-marks, patented articles, and the rights of manufacturing firms and corporations. The formulating into treaties of the recommendations thus adopted is receiving the attention which it merits.

The protection of submarine cables is a subject now under consideration by an international conference at Paris. Believing that it is clearly the true policy of this Government to favor the neutralization of this means of intercourse, I requested our minister to France to attend the convention as a delegate. I also designated two of our eminent scientists to attend as our representatives at the meeting of an international committee at Paris, for considering the adoption of a common unit to measure electric force.

In view of the frequent occurrence of conferences for the consideration of important matters of common interest to civilized nations, I respectfully suggest that the Executive be invested by Congress with discretionary powers to send delegates to such conventions, and that provision be made to defray the expenses incident thereto.

The difference between the United States and Spain as to the effect of a judgment and certificate of naturalization has not yet been adjusted ; but it is hoped and believed that negotiations now in progress will result in the establishment of the position which seems to this Government so reasonable and just.

I have already called the attention of Congress to the fact that in the ports of Spain and its colonies onerous fines have lately been imposed upon vessels of the United States for trivial technical offenses against local regulations. Efforts for the abatement of these exactions have thus far proved unsuccessful.

I regret to inform you also that the fees demanded by Spanish consuls in American ports are in some cases so large, when compared with the value of the cargo, as to amount in effect to a considerable export duty, and that our remonstrances in this regard have not as yet received the attention which they seem to deserve.

The German Government has invited the United States to participate in an international exhibition of domestic cattle, to be held at Hamburg in July, 1883. If this country is to be represented, it is important that, in the early days of this session, Congress should make a suitable appropriation for that purpose.

The death of Mr. Marsh, our late minister to Italy, has evoked from that Government expressions of profound respect for his exalted character and for his honorable career in the diplomatic service of his country. The Italian Government has raised a question as to the propriety of recognizing in his dual capacity the representative of this country recently accredited both as secretary of legation and as consul-general at Rome. He has been received as secretary, but his exequatur as consul-general has thus far been withheld.

The extradition convention with Belgium, which has been in operation since 1874, has been lately supplanted by another. The Senate has signified its approval, and ratifications have been duly exchanged between the contracting countries. To the list of extraditable crimes has been added that of the assassination or attempted assassination of the chief of the state.

Negotiations have been opened with Switzerland looking to a settlement by treaty of the question whether its citizens can renounce their allegiance and become citizens of the United States without obtaining the consent of the Swiss Government.

I am glad to inform you that the immigration of paupers and criminals from certain of the cantons of Switzerland has substantially ceased and is no longer sanctioned by the authorities.

The consideration of this subject prompts the suggestion that the act of August 3, 1882, which has for its object the return of foreign convicts to their own country, should be so modified as not to be open to the interpretation that it affects the extradition of criminals on preferred charges of crime.

The Ottoman Porte has not yet assented to the interpretation which this Government has put upon the treaty of 1830 relative to its jurisdictional rights in Turkey. It may well be, however, that this difference will be adjusted by a general revision of the system of jurisdiction of the United States in the countries of the East—a subject to which your attention has been already called by the Secretary of State.

In the interest of justice towards China and Japan, I trust that the question of the return of the indemnity fund to the Governments of those countries will reach, at the present session, the satisfactory solution which I have already recommended, and which has recently been foreshadowed by Congressional discussion.

The treaty lately concluded with Corea awaits the action of the Senate.

During the late disturbance in Egypt the timely presence of American vessels served as a protection to the persons and property of many of our own citizens and of citizens of other countries, whose Governments have expressed their thanks for this assistance.

The recent legislation restricting immigration of laborers from China has given rise to the question whether Chinese proceeding to or from another country may lawfully pass through our own.

Construing the act of May 6, 1882, in connection with the treaty of November 7, 1880, the restriction would seem to be limited to Chinese immigrants coming to the United States as laborers, and would not forbid a mere transit across our territory. I ask the attention of Congress to the subject for such action, if any, as may be deemed advisable.

This Government has recently had occasion to manifest its interest in the Republic of Liberia by seeking to aid the amicable settlement of the boundary dispute now pending between that republic and the British possession of Sierra Leone.

The reciprocity treaty with Hawaii will become terminable after September 9, 1883, on twelve months' notice by either party. While certain provisions of that compact may have proved onerous, its existence has fostered commercial relations which it is important to preserve. I suggest, therefore, that early consideration be given to such modifications of the treaty as seem to be demanded by the interests of our people.

In view of our increasing trade with both Hayti and Santo Domingo I advise that provision be made for diplomatic intercourse with the latter, by enlarging the scope of the mission at Port au Prince.

I regret that certain claims of American citizens against the Government of Hayti have thus far been urged unavailingly.

A recent agreement with Mexico provides for the crossing of the frontier by the armed forces of either country in pursuit of hostile Indians. In my message of last year I called attention to the prevalent lawlessness upon the borders and to the necessity of legislation for its suppression. I again invite the attention of Congress to the subject.

A partial relief from these mischiefs has been sought in a convention, which now awaits the approval of the Senate, as does also another touching the establishment of the international boundary between the United States and Mexico. If the latter is ratified, the action of Congress will be required for establishing suitable commissions of survey. The boundary dispute between Mexico and Guatemala, which led this Government to proffer its friendly counsels to both parties, has been amicably settled.

No change has occurred in our relations with Venezuela. I again invoke your action in the matter of the pending awards against that republic to which reference was made by a special message from the Executive at your last session.

An invitation has been received from the Government of Venezuela to send representatives in July, 1883, to Caracas, for participating in the centennial celebration of the birth of Bolivar, the founder of South American independence. In connection with this event it is designed to commence the erection at Caracas of a statue of Washington, and to conduct an industrial exhibition which will be open to American products. I recommend that the United States be represented, and that suitable provision be made therefor.

The elevation of the grade of our mission in Central America to the plenipotentiary rank, which was authorized by Congress at its late session, has been since effected.

The war between Peru and Bolivia on the one side and Chili on the other began more than three years ago. On the occupation by Chili in 1880 of all the littoral territory of Bolivia, negotiations for peace were conducted under the direction of the United States. The allies refused to concede any territory, but Chili has since become master of the whole coast of both countries and of the capital of Peru. A year since, as you have already been advised by correspondence transmitted to you in January last, this Government sent a special mission to the belligerent powers to express the hope that Chili would be disposed to accept a money indemnity for the expenses of the war and to relinquish her demand for a portion of the territory of her antagonist.

This recommendation, which Chili declined to follow, this Government did not assume to enforce; nor can it be enforced without resort to measures which would be in keeping neither with the temper of our people nor with the spirit of our institutions.

The power of Peru no longer extends over its whole territory, and, in the event of our interference to dictate peace, would need to be supplemented by the armies and navies of the United States. Such interference would almost inevitably lead to the establishment of a protectorate—a result utterly at odds with our past policy, injurious to our present interests, and full of embarrassments for the future.

For effecting the termination of hostilities upon terms at once just to the victorious nation and generous to its adversaries, this Government has spared no efforts save such as might involve the complications which I have indicated.

It is greatly to be deplored that Chili seems resolved to exact such rigorous conditions of peace and indisposed to submit to arbitration the terms of an amicable settlement. No peace is likely to be lasting that is not sufficiently equitable and just to command the approval of other nations.

About a year since, invitations were extended to the nations of this continent to send representatives to a peace congress to assemble at Washington in November, 1882. The time of meeting was fixed at a period then remote, in the hope, as the invitation itself declared, that in the mean time the disturbances between the South American republics would be adjusted. As that expectation seemed unlikely to be realized, I asked in April last for an expression of opinion from the two houses of Congress as to the advisability of holding the proposed convention at the time appointed. This action was prompted in part by doubts which mature reflection had suggested whether the diplomatic usage and traditions of the Government did not make it fitting that the Executive should consult the representatives of the people before pursuing a line of policy somewhat novel in its character, and far-reaching in its possible consequences. In view of the fact that no action was taken by Congress in the premises and that no provision had been made for necessary expenses, I subsequently decided to postpone the convocation, and so notified the several Governments which had been invited to attend.

I am unwilling to dismiss this subject without assuring you of my support of any measures the wisdom of Congress may devise for the promotion of peace on this continent and throughout the world, and I trust that the time is nigh when, with the universal assent of civilized peoples, all international differences shall be determined without resort to arms by the benignant processes of arbitration.

Changes have occurred in the diplomatic representation of several foreign powers during the past year. New ministers from the Argentine Republic, Austria-Hungary, Brazil, Chili, China, France, Japan, Mexico, the Netherlands, and Russia have presented their credentials. The missions of Denmark and Venezuela at this capital have been raised in grade. Switzerland has created a plenipotentiary mission to this Government, and an embassy from Madagascar and a minister from Siam will shortly arrive.

Our diplomatic intercourse has been enlarged by the establishment of relations with the new Kingdom of Servia, by the creation of a mission to Siam, and by the restoration of the mission to Greece. The Shah of Persia has expressed his gratification that a chargé d'affaires will shortly be sent to that country, where the rights of our citizens have been hitherto courteously guarded by the representatives of Great Britain.

I renew my recommendation of such legislation as will place the United States in harmony with other maritime powers with respect to the international rules for the prevention of collisions at sea.

In conformity with your joint resolution of the 3d of August last, I have directed the Secretary of State to address foreign Governments in respect to a proposed conference for considering the subject of the universal adoption of a common prime meridian to be used in the reckoning of longitude and in the regulation of time throughout the civilized world. Their replies will, in due time, be laid before you.

An agreement was reached at Paris in 1875 between the principal powers for the interchange of official publications through the medium of their respective foreign departments.

The admirable system which has been built up by the enterprise of the Smithsonian Institution affords a practical basis for our co-operation in this scheme, and an arrangement has been effected by which that institution will perform the necessary labor, under the direction of the Department of State. A reasonable compensation therefor should be provided by law.

A clause in the act making appropriations for the diplomatic and consular service contemplates the reorganization of both branches of such service on a salaried basis, leaving fees to inure to the benefit of the Treasury. I cordially favor such a project, as likely to correct abuses in the present system. The Secretary of State will present to you at an early day a plan for such reorganization.

A full and interesting exhibit of the operations of the Treasury Department is afforded by the report of the Secretary.

It appears that the ordinary revenues from all sources for the fiscal year ended June 30, 1882, were as follows :

From customs..	$220,410,730 25
From internal revenue	146,497,595 45
From sales of public lands....................................	4,753,140 37
From tax on circulation and deposits of national banks...	8,956,794 45
From repayment of interest by Pacific Railway Companies	840,554 37
From sinking fund for Pacific Railway Companies..	796,271 42
From customs fees, fines, penalties, &c	1,343,348 00
From fees—consular, letters patent, and lands.....	2,638,990 97
From proceeds of sales of Government property..	314,959 85
From profits on coinage, bullion deposits, and assays................................	4,116,693 73
From Indian trust funds	5,705,243 22
From deposits by individuals for surveying public lands	2,052,306 36

From revenues of the District of Columbia.........	$1,715,176 41
From miscellaneous sources	3,383,445 43
Total ordinary receipts.........................	.403,525,250 28

The ordinary expenditures for the same period were—

For civil expenses..	$18,042,386 42
For foreign intercourse	1,307,583 19
For Indians...	9,736,747 40
For pensions...	61,345,193 95
For the military establishment, including river and harbor improvements, and arsenals...........	43,570,494 19
For the naval establishment, including vessels, machinery, and improvements at navy-yards....	15,032,046 26
For miscellaneous expenditures, including public buildings, light-houses, and collecting the revenue...	34,539,237 50
For expenditures on account of the District of Columbia	3,330,543 87
For interest on the public debt.......................	71,077,206 79
Total ordinary expenditures....................	257,981,439 57
Leaving a surplus revenue of..........................	145,543,810 71
Which, with an amount drawn from the cash balance in the Treasury of.............	20,737,694 84
Making	166,281,505 55

Was applied to the redemption—

Of bonds for the sinking fund	60,079,150 00
Of fractional currency for the sinking fund......	58,705 55
Of loan of July and August, 1861.................	62,572,050 00
Of loan of March, 1863.............................	4,472,900 00
Of funded loan of 1881	37,194,450 00
Of loan of 1858......................................	1,000 00
Of loan of February, 1861	303,000 00
Of five-twenties of 1862.............................	2,100 00
Of five-twenties of 1864.............................	7,400 00
Of five-twenties of 1865.............................	6,500 00

Of ten-forties of 1864.....	$254,550 00
Of consols of 1865..	86,450 00
Of consols of 1867.......................................	408,250 00
Of consols of 1868................	141,400 00
Of Oregon war debt.....................................	675,250 00
Of old demand, compound-interest, and other notes ....,	18,350 00
	166,281,505 55

The foreign commerce of the United States during the last fiscal year, including imports and exports of merchandise and specie, was as follows:

Exports: Merchandise..........	$750,542,257
Specie....................................	49,417,479
Total...............	799,959,736
Imports: Merchandise...........................	724,639,574
Specie ....,.....................	42,472,390
Total.......................................	767,111,964
Excess of exports over imports of merchandise.....	25,902,683

This excess is less than it has been before for any of the previous six years, as appears by the following table:

Year ended June 30—	Excess of exports over imports of merchandise.
1876..	$79,643,481
1877..	151,152,094
1878..	257,814,234
1879..	264,661,666
1880..	167,683,912
1881..	259,712,718
1882..	25,902,683

During the year there have been organized 171 national banks, and of those institutions there are now in operation 2,269, a larger number than ever before. The value of their notes in active circulation on July 1, 1882, was $324,656,458.

I commend to your attention the Secretary's views in respect to the likelihood of a serious contraction of this circulation, and to the modes by which that result may, in his judgment, be averted.

In respect to the coinage of silver dollars and the retirement of silver certificates I have seen nothing to alter but much to confirm the sentiments to which I gave expression last year.

A comparison between the respective amounts of silver-dollar circulation on November 1, 1881, and on November 1, 1882, shows a slight increase of a million and a half of dollars. But during the interval there had been in the whole number coined an increase of twenty-six millions. Of the one hundred and twenty-eight millions thus far minted, little more than thirty-five millions are in circulation. The mass of accumulated coin has grown so great that the vault room at present available for storage is scarcely sufficient to contain it. It is not apparent why it is desirable to continue this coinage, now so enormously in excess of the public demand.

As to the silver certificates, in addition to the grounds which seemed last year to justify their retirement may be mentioned the effect which is likely to ensue from the supply of gold certificates, for whose issuance Congress recently made provision, and which are now in active circulation.

You cannot fail to note with interest the discussion by the Secretary as to the necessity of providing by legislation some mode of freeing the Treasury of an excess of assets, in the event that Congress fails to reach an early agreement for the reduction of taxation.

I heartily approve the Secretary's recommendation of immediate and extensive reductions in the annual revenues of the Government.

It will be remembered that I urged upon the attention of Congress at its last session the importance of relieving the industry and enterprise of the country from the pressure of unnecessary taxation. It is one of the tritest maxims of political economy that all taxes are burdensome, however wisely and prudently imposed. And though there have always been among our people wide differences of sentiment as to the best methods of raising the national revenues, and, indeed, as to the principles upon which taxation should be based, there has been substantial accord in the doctrine that only such taxes ought to be levied as are necessary for a wise and economical administration of the Government. Of late the public revenues have far exceeded that limit, and unless checked by appropriate legislation such excess will continue to increase from year to year. For the fiscal year ended June 30, 1881, the surplus revenue amounted to one hundred millions of dollars; for the fiscal year ended on the 30th of June last the surplus was more than one hundred and forty-five millions.

The report of the Secretary shows what disposition has been made of these moneys. They have not only answered the requirements of the sinking fund, but have afforded a large balance applicable to other reductions of the public debt.

But I renew the expression of my conviction that such rapid extinguishment of the national indebtedness as is now taking place is by no means a cause for congratulation; it is a cause rather for serious apprehension.

If it continues, it must speedily be followed by one of the evil results so clearly set forth in the report of the Secretary.

Either the surplus must lie idle in the Treasury, or the Government will be forced to buy, at market rates, its bonds not then redeemable, and which, under such circumstances, cannot fail to command an enormous premium, or the swollen revenues will be devoted to extravagant expenditure, which, as experience has taught, is ever the bane of an overflowing treasury.

It was made apparent in the course of the animated discussions which this question aroused at the last session of Congress that the policy of diminishing the revenue by reducing taxation commanded the general approval of the members of both houses.

I regret that because of conflicting views as to the best methods by which that policy should be made operative none of its benefits have as yet been reaped.

In fulfillment of what I deem my constitutional duty, but with little hope that I can make valuable contribution to this vexed question, I shall proceed to intimate briefly my own views in relation to it.

Upon the showing of our financial condition at the close of the last fiscal year, I felt justified in recommending to Congress the abolition of all internal-revenue taxes except those upon tobacco in its various forms and upon distilled spirits and fermented liquors; and except also the special tax upon the manufacturers of and dealers in such articles.

I venture now to suggest that, unless it shall be ascertained that the probable expenditures of the Government for the coming year have been underestimated, all internal taxes, save those which relate to distilled spirits, can be prudently abrogated.

Such a course, if accompanied by a simplification of the machinery of collection, which would then be easy of accomplishment, might reasonably be expected to result in diminishing the cost of such collection by at least two millions and a half of dollars, and in the retirement from office of from fifteen hundred to two thousand persons.

The system of excise duties has never commended itself to the favor of the American people, and has never been resorted to except for supplying deficiencies in the Treasury when, by reason of special exigencies, the duties on imports have proved inadequate for the needs of the Government. The sentiment of the country doubtless demands that the present excise tax shall be abolished as soon as such a course can be safely pursued.

It seems to me, however, that, for various reasons, so sweeping a measure as the total abolition of internal taxes would for the present be an unwise step.

Two of these reasons are deserving of special mention :

First, it is by no means clear that even if the existing system of duties on imports is continued without modification, those duties alone will yield sufficient revenue for all the needs of the Government. It is estimated that one hundred millions of dollars will be required for pensions during the coming year, and it may well be doubted whether the maximum annual demand for that object has yet been reached. Uncertainty upon this question would alone justify, in my judgment, the retention for the present of that portion of the system of internal revenue which is least objectionable to the people.

Second, a total abolition of excise taxes would almost inevitably prove a serious if not an insurmountable obstacle to a thorough

10*

revision of the tariff and to any considerable reduction in import duties.

The present tariff system is in many respects unjust. It makes unequal distributions both of its burdens and its benefits. This fact was practically recognized by a majority of each house of Congress in the passage of the act creating the Tariff Commission. The report of that Commission will be placed before you at the beginning of this session, and will, I trust, afford you such information as to the condition and prospects of the various commercial, agricultural, manufacturing, mining, and other interests of the country and contain such suggestions for statutory revision as will practically aid your action upon this important subject.

The revenue from customs for the fiscal year ended June 30, 1879, amounted to $137,000,000.

It has in the three succeeding years reached, first, $186,000,000; then, $198,000,000; and finally, as has been already stated, $220,000,000.

The income from this source for the fiscal year which will end on June 30, 1883, will doubtless be considerably in excess of the sum last mentioned.

If the tax on domestic spirits is to be retained, it is plain therefore that large reductions from the customs revenue are entirely feasible. While recommending this reduction I am far from advising the abandonment of the policy of so discriminating in the adjustment of details as to afford aid and protection to domestic labor. But the present system should be so revised as to equalize the public burden among all classes and occupations, and bring it into closer harmony with the present needs of industry.

Without entering into minute detail, which, under present circumstances, is quite unnecessary, I recommend an enlargement of the free list so as to include within it the numerous articles which yield inconsiderable revenue, a simplification of the complex and inconsistent schedule of duties upon certain manufactures, particularly those of cotton, iron, and steel, and a substantial reduction of the duties upon those articles, and upon sugar, molasses, silk, wool, and woolen goods.

If a general revision of the tariff shall be found to be impracticable *at this* session, I express the hope that at least some of the more conspicuous inequalities of the present law may be corrected before your final adjournment. One of them is specially referred to by the Secretary. In view of a recent decision of the Supreme Court, the necessity of amending the law by which the Dutch standard of color is adopted as the test of the saccharine strength of sugars is too obvious to require comment.

From the report of the Secretary of War it appears that the only outbreaks of Indians during the past year occurred in Arizona and in the southwestern part of New Mexico. They were promptly quelled, and the quiet which has prevailed in all other parts of the country has permitted such an addition to be made to the military force in the region endangered by the Apaches that there is little reason to apprehend trouble in the future.

Those parts of the Secretary's report which relate to our sea-coast defenses and their armament suggest the gravest reflections. Our existing fortifications are notoriously inadequate to the defense of the great harbors and cities for whose protection they were built.

The question of providing an armament suited to our present necessities has been the subject of consideration by a board, whose report was transmitted to Congress at the last session. Pending the consideration of that report, the War Department has taken no steps for the manufacture or conversion of any heavy cannon, but the Secretary expresses the hope that authority and means to begin that important work will be soon provided. I invite the attention of Congress to the propriety of making more adequate provision for arming and equipping the militia than is afforded by the act of 1808, which is still upon the statute-book. The matter has already been the subject of discussion in the Senate, and a bill which seeks to supply the deficiencies of existing laws is now upon its calendar.

The Secretary of War calls attention to an embarrassment growing out of the recent act of Congress making the retirement of officers of the Army compulsory at the age of sixty-four. The act of 1878 is still in force, which limits to four hundred the number of those who can be retired for disability or upon their own application. The two acts, when construed together, seem to forbid the relieving, even for absolute incapacity, of officers who do not fall within the purview of the later statute, save at such times as there chance to be less than four hundred names on the retired list. There are now four hundred and twenty. It is not likely that Congress intended this result, and I concur with the Secretary, that the law ought to be amended.

The grounds that impelled me to withhold my signature from the bill entitled "An act making appropriations for the construction, repair, and preservation of certain works on rivers and harbors," which became a law near the close of your last session, prompt me to express the hope that no similar measure will be deemed necessary during the present session of Congress. Indeed, such a measure would now be open to a serious objection in addition to that which was lately urged upon your attention. I am informed by the Secretary of War that the greater portion of the sum appropriated for the various items specified in that act remains unexpended.

Of the new works which it authorized, expenses have been incurred upon two only, for which the total appropriation was $210,-000. The present available balance is disclosed by the following table:

Amount of appropriation by act of August 2, 1882	$18,738,875
Amount of appropriation by act of June 19, 1882	10,000
Amount of appropriation for payments to J. B. Eads	304,000
Unexpended balance of former appropriations	4,738,263
	23,791,138
Less amount drawn from Treasury between July 1, 1882, and November 30, 1882	6,056,194
	17,734,944

It is apparent by this exhibit that, so far as concerns most of the items to which the act of August 2, 1882, relates, there can be no need of further appropriations until after the close of the present session. If, however, any action should seem to be necessary in respect to particular objects, it will be entirely feasible to provide for those objects by appropriate legislation. It is possible, for example, that a delay until the assembling of the next Congress to make additional provision for the Mississippi River improvements might be attended with serious consequences. If such should appear to be the case, a just bill relating to that subject would command my approval.

This leads me to offer a suggestion which I trust will commend itself to the wisdom of Congress. Is it not advisable that grants of considerable sums of money for diverse and independent schemes of internal improvement should be made the subjects of separate and distinct legislative enactments? It will scarcely be gainsaid, even by those who favor the most liberal expenditures for such purposes as are sought to be accomplished by what is commonly called the river and harbor bill, that the practice of grouping in such a bill appropriations for a great diversity of objects, widely separated, either in their nature or in the locality with which they are concerned, or in both, is one which is much to be deprecated unless it is irremediable. It inevitably tends to secure the success of the bill as a whole, though many of the items, if separately considered, could scarcely fail of rejection. By the adoption of the course I have recommended, every member of Congress, whenever opportunity should arise for giving his influence and vote for meritorious appropriations, would be enabled so to do without being called upon to sanction others undeserving his approval. So also would the Executive be afforded thereby full opportunity to exercise his constitutional prerogative of opposing whatever appropriations seemed to him objectionable, without imperiling the success of others which commended themselves to his judgment.

It may be urged in opposition to these suggestions that the number of works of internal improvement which are justly entitled to governmental aid is so great as to render impracticable separate appropriation bills therefor, or even for such comparatively limited number as make disposition of large sums of money. This objection may be well founded, and, whether it be or not, the advantages which would be likely to ensue from the adoption of the course I have recommended may perhaps be more effectually attained by another, which I respectfully submit to Congress as an alternative proposition.

It is provided by the constitutions of fourteen of our States that the Executive may disapprove any item or items of a bill appropriating money; whereupon the part of the bill approved shall be law, and the part disapproved shall fail to become law, unless repassed according to the provisions prescribed for the passage of bills over the veto of the Executive. The States wherein some such provision as the foregoing is a part of the fundamental law are, Alabama, California, Colorado, Florida, Georgia, Louisiana, Minnesota, Missouri, Nebraska, New Jersey, New York, Pennsylvania, Texas, and West Virginia. I commend to your careful consideration the question whether an amendment of the Federal Constitution in the particular indicated would not afford the best remedy for what is often a grave embarrassment both to members of Congress and to the Executive, and is sometimes a serious public mischief.

The report of the Secretary of the Navy states the movements of the various squadrons during the year, in home and foreign waters, where our officers and seamen, with such ships as we possess, have continued to illustrate the high character and excellent discipline of the naval organization.

On the 21st of December, 1881, information was received that the exploring steamer Jeannette had been crushed and abandoned in the Arctic Ocean. The officers and crew, after a journey over the ice, embarked in three boats for the coast of Siberia. One of the parties, under the command of Chief Engineer George W. Melville, reached the land, and, falling in with the natives, was saved. Another, under Lieutenant-Commander De Long, landed in a barren region near the mouth of the Lena River. After six weeks had elapsed all but two of the number had died from fatigue and starvation. No tidings have been received from the party in the third boat, under the command of Lieutenant Chipp, but a long and fruitless investigation leaves little doubt that all its members perished at sea. As a slight tribute to their heroism I give in this communication the names of the gallant men who sacrificed their lives on this expedition: Lieutenant-Commander George W. De Long, Surgeon James M. Ambler, Jerome J. Collins, Hans Halmer Erichsen, Heinrich H. Kaacke, George W. Boyd, Walter Lee, Adolph Dressler, Carl A. Görtz, Nelse Iverson, the cook Ah Sam, and the Indian Alexy. The officers and men in the missing boat were Lieutenant Charles W. Chipp, commanding; William Dunbar, Alfred Sweetman, Walter Sharvell, Albert C. Kuehne, Edward Star, Henry D. Warren, and Peter E. Johnson.

Lieutenant Giles B. Harber and Master William H. Scheutze are now bringing home the remains of Lieutenant De Long and his comrades, in pursuance of the directions of Congress.

The Rodgers, fitted out for the relief of the Jeannette, in accordance with the act of Congress of March 3, 1881, sailed from San Francisco June 16, under the command of Lieutenant Robert M. Berry. On November 30 she was accidentally destroyed by fire, while in winter quarters in Saint Lawrence Bay, but the officers and crew succeeded in escaping to the shore. Lieutenant Berry and one of his officers, after making a search for the Jeannette along the coast of Siberia, fell in with Chief Engineer Melville's party, and returned home by way of Europe. The other officers and the crew of the Rodgers were brought from Saint Lawrence Bay by the whaling steamer North Star. Master Charles F. Putnam, who had been placed in charge of a depot of supplies at Cape Serdze, returning to his post from Saint Lawrence Bay across the ice in a blinding snow-storm, was carried out to sea and lost, notwithstanding all efforts to rescue him.

It appears by the Secretary's report that the available naval force of the United States consists of thirty-seven cruisers, fourteen single-turreted monitors, built during the rebellion, a large number of smooth-bore guns and Parrott rifles, and eighty-seven rifled cannon.

The cruising vessels should be gradually replaced by iron or steel ships, the monitors by modern armored vessels, and the armament by high-power rifled guns.

The reconstruction of our Navy, which was recommended in my last message, was begun by Congress authorizing, in its recent act, the construction of two large unarmored steel vessels of the character recommended by the late Naval Advisory Board, and subject to the final approval of a new advisory board to be organized as provided by that act. I call your attention to the recommendation of the Secretary and the board, that authority be given to construct two more cruisers of smaller dimensions, and one fleet dispatch vessel, and that appropriations be made for high-power rifled cannon, for the torpedo service, and for other harbor defenses.

Pending the consideration by Congress of the policy to be here-after adopted in conducting the eight large navy-yards and their expensive establishments, the Secretary advocates the reduction of expenditures therefor to the lowest possible amounts.

For the purpose of affording the officers and seamen of the Navy opportunities for exercise and discipline in their profession, under appropriate control and direction, the Secretary advises that the Light-House Service and Coast Survey be transferred, as now organ-ized, from the Treasury to the Navy Department; and he also sug-gests, for the reasons which he assigns, that a similar transfer may wisely be made of the cruising revenue vessels.

The Secretary forcibly depicts the intimate connection and inter-dependence of the Navy and the commercial marine, and invites attention to the continued decadence of the latter and the corre-sponding transfer of our growing commerce to foreign bottoms.

This subject is one of the utmost importance to the national wel-fare. Methods of reviving American ship-building and of restoring the United States flag in the ocean carrying trade should receive the immediate attention of Congress. We have mechanical skill and abundant material for the manufacture of modern iron steamships in fair competition with our commercial rivals. Our disadvantage in building ships is the greater cost of labor, and in sailing them, higher taxes, and greater interest on capital, while the ocean high-ways are already monopolized by our formidable competitors. These obstacles should in some way be overcome, and for our rapid com-munication with foreign lands we should not continue to depend wholly upon vessels built in the yards of other countries and sailing under foreign flags. With no United States steamers on the prin-cipal ocean lines or in any foreign ports, our facilities for extending our commerce are greatly restricted, while the nations which build and sail the ships and carry the mails and passengers obtain thereby conspicuous advantages in increasing their trade.

The report of the Postmaster-General gives evidence of the satis-factory condition of that Department, and contains many valuable data and accompanying suggestions which cannot fail to be of in-terest.

The information which it affords that the receipts for the fiscal year have exceeded the expenditures must be very gratifying to Congress and to the people of the country.

As matters which may fairly claim particular attention, I refer you to his observations in reference to the advisability of changing the present basis for fixing salaries and allowances, of extending the money-order system, and of enlarging the functions of the postal establishment so as to put under its control the telegraph system of the country, though from this last and most important recommendation I must withhold my concurrence.

At the last session of Congress several bills were introduced into the House of Representatives for the reduction of letter postage to the rate of two cents per half ounce.

I have given much study and reflection to this subject, and am thoroughly persuaded that such a reduction would be for the best interests of the public.

It has been the policy of the Government from its foundation to defray, as far as possible, the expenses of carrying the mails by a direct tax in the form of postage. It has never been claimed, however, that this service ought to be productive of a net revenue.

As has been stated already, the report of the Postmaster-General shows that there is now a very considerable surplus in his Department, and that henceforth the receipts are likely to increase at a much greater ratio than the necessary expenditures. Unless some change is made in the existing laws the profits of the postal service will in a very few years swell the revenues of the Government many millions of dollars. The time seems auspicious, therefore, for some reduction in the rates of postage. In what shall that reduction consist?

A review of the legislation which has been had upon this subject during the last thirty years discloses that domestic letters constitute the only class of mail matter which has never been favored by a substantial reduction of rates. I am convinced that the burden of maintaining the service falls most unequally upon that class, and that more than any other it is entitled to present relief.

That such relief may be extended without detriment to other public interests will be discovered upon reviewing the results of former reductions.

Immediately prior to the act of 1845, the postage upon a letter composed of a single sheet was as follows:

If conveyed	Cents.
30 miles or less...	6
Between 30 and 80 miles.......................................	10
Between 80 and 150 miles....................................	12½
Between 150 and 400 miles.....	18¾
Over 400 miles...............	25

By the act of 1845 the postage upon a single letter conveyed for any distance under·300 miles was fixed at five cents, and for any greater distance at ten cents.

By the act of 1851 it was provided that a single letter, if prepaid. should be carried any distance not exceeding three thousand miles for three cents and any greater distance for six cents.

It will be noticed that both of these reductions were of a radical character and relatively quite as important as that which is now proposed.

In each case there ensued a temporary loss of revenue, but a sudden and large influx of business, which substantially repaired that loss within three years.

Unless the experience of past legislation in this country and elsewhere goes for naught, it may be safely predicted that the stimulus of 33⅓ per centum reduction in the tax for carriage would at once increase the number of letters consigned to the mails.

The advantages of secrecy would lead to a very general substitution of sealed packets for postal cards and open circulars, and in divers other ways the volume of first-class matter would be enormously augmented. Such increase amounted in England, in the first year after the adoption of penny postage, to more than 125 per cent.

As a result of careful estimates, the details of which cannot be here set out, I have become convinced that the deficiency for the first year after the proposed reduction would not exceed 7 per cent. of the expenditures, or $3,000,000, while the deficiency after the reduction of 1845 was more than 14 per cent., and after that of 1851 was 27 per cent.

Another interesting comparison is afforded by statistics furnished me by the Post-Office Department.

The act of 1845 was passed in face of the fact that there existed a deficiency of more than $30,000. That of 1851 was encouraged by the slight surplus of $132,000. The excess of revenue in the next fiscal year is likely to be $3,500,000.

If Congress should approve these suggestions it may be deemed desirable to supply to some extent the deficiency which must for a time result, by increasing the charge for carrying merchandise, which is now only sixteen cents per pound. But even without such an increase I am confident that the receipts under the diminished rates would equal the expenditures after the lapse of three or four years.

The report of the Department of Justice brings anew to your notice the necessity of enlarging the present system of Federal jurisprudence so as effectually to answer the requirements of the ever-increasing litigation with which it is called upon to deal.

The Attorney-General renews the suggestions of his predecessor that in the interests of justice better provision than the existing laws afford should be made in certain judicial districts for fixing the fees of witnesses and jurors.

In my message of December last I referred to pending criminal proceedings growing out of alleged frauds in what is known as the star-route service of the Post-Office Department, and advised you that I had enjoined upon the Attorney-General and associate counsel, to whom the interests of the Government were intrusted, the duty of prosecuting with the utmost vigor of the law all persons who might be found chargeable with those offenses. A trial of one of these cases has since occurred. It occupied for many weeks the attention of the supreme court of this District, and was conducted with great zeal and ability. It resulted in a disagreement of the jury, but the cause has been again placed upon the calendar and will shortly be retried. If any guilty persons shall finally escape punishment for their offenses it will not be for lack of diligent and earnest efforts on the part of the prosecution.

I trust that some agreement may be reached which will speedily enable Congress, with the concurrence of the Executive, to afford the commercial community the benefits of a national bankrupt law.

The report of the Secretary of the Interior, with its accompanying documents, presents a full statement of the varied operations of that Department. In respect to Indian affairs nothing has occurred which has changed or seriously modified the views to which I devoted much space in a former communication to Congress. I renew the recommendations therein contained as to extending to the Indian the protection of the law, allotting land in severalty to such as desire it, and making suitable provision for the education of youth. Such provision, as the Secretary forcibly maintains, will prove unavailing unless it is broad enough to include all those who are able and willing to make use of it, and should not solely relate to intellectual training, but also to instruction in such manual labor and simple industrial arts as can be made practically available.

Among other important subjects which are included within the Secretary's report, and which will doubtless furnish occasion for Congressional action, may be mentioned the neglect of the railroad companies to which large grants of land were made by the acts of 1862 and 1864 to take title thereto, and their consequent inequitable exemption from local taxation.

No survey of our material condition can fail to suggest inquiries as to the moral and intellectual progress of the people.

The Census returns disclose an alarming state of illiteracy in certain portions of the country where the provision for schools is grossly inadequate. It is a momentous question for the decision of Congress whether immediate and substantial aid should not be extended by the General Government for supplementing the efforts of private beneficence and of State and Territorial legislation in behalf of education.

The regulation of inter-state commerce has already been the subject of your deliberations. One of the incidents of the marvelous extension of the railway system of the country has been the adoption of such measures by the corporations which own or control the roads as has tended to impair the advantages of healthful competition and to make hurtful discriminations in the adjustment of freightage.

These inequalities have been corrected in several of the States by appropriate legislation, the effect of which is necessarily restricted to the limits of their own territory.

So far as such mischiefs affect commerce between the States, or between any one of the States and a foreign country, they are subjects of national concern, and Congress alone can afford relief.

The results which have thus far attended the enforcement of the recent statute for the suppression of polygamy in the Territories are reported by the Secretary of the Interior. It is not probable that any additional legislation in this regard will be deemed desirable until the effect of existing laws shall be more closely observed and studied.

I congratulate you that the commissioners under whose supervision those laws have been put in operation are encouraged to believe that the evil at which they are aimed may be suppressed without resort to such radical measures as in some quarters have been thought indispensable for success.

The close relation of the General Government to the Territories preparing to be great States may well engage your special attention. It is there that the Indian disturbances mainly occur and that polygamy has found room for its growth. I cannot doubt that a careful survey of Territorial legislation would be of the highest utility. Life and property would become more secure. The liability of outbreaks between Indians and whites would be lessened. The public domain would be more securely guarded and better progress be made in the instruction of the young.

Alaska is still without any form of civil government. If means were provided for the education of its people and for the protection of their lives and property the immense resources of the region would invite permanent settlements and open new fields for industry and enterprise.

The report of the Commissioner of Agriculture presents an account of the labors of that Department during the past year, and includes information of much interest to the general public.

The condition of the forests of the country and the wasteful manner in which their destruction is taking place give cause for serious apprehension. Their action in protecting the earth's surface, in modifying the extremes of climate, and in regulating and sustaining the flow of springs and streams is now well understood, and their importance in relation to the growth and prosperity of the country cannot be safely disregarded. They are fast disappearing before destructive fires and the legitimate requirements of our increasing population, and their total extinction cannot be long delayed unless better methods than now prevail shall be adopted for their protection and cultivation. The attention of Congress is invited to the necessity of additional legislation to secure the preservation of the valuable forests still remaining on the public domain, especially in the extreme Western States and Territories, where the necessity for their preservation is greater than in less mountainous regions, and where the prevailing dryness of the climate renders their restoration, if they are once destroyed, well nigh impossible.

The communication which I made to Congress at its first session in December last contained a somewhat full statement of my sentiments in relation to the principles and rules which ought to govern appointments to public service.

Referring to the various plans which had theretofore been the subject of discussion in the National Legislature (plans which in the main were modeled upon the system which obtains in Great Britain, but which lacked certain of the prominent features whereby that system is distinguished), I felt bound to intimate my doubts whether they, or any of them, would afford adequate remedy for the evils which they aimed to correct.

I declared, nevertheless, that if the proposed measures should prove acceptable to Congress, they would receive the unhesitating support of the Executive.

Since these suggestions were submitted for your consideration there has been no legislation upon the subject to which they relate, but there has meanwhile been an increase in the public interest in that subject, and the people of the country, apparently without distinction of party, have in various ways, and upon frequent occasions, given expression to their earnest wish for prompt and definite action. In my judgment, such action should no longer be postponed.

I may add that my own sense of its pressing importance has been quickened by observation of a practical phase of the matter, to which attention has more than once been called by my predecessors.

The civil list now comprises about one hundred thousand persons, far the larger part of whom must, under the terms of the Constitution, be selected by the President either directly or through his own appointees.

In the early years of the administration of the Government, the personal direction of appointments to the civil service may not have been an irksome task for the Executive; but, now that the burden has increased fully a hundred-fold, it has become greater than he ought to bear, and it necessarily diverts his time and attention from the proper discharge of other duties no less delicate and responsible, and which, in the very nature of things, cannot be delegated to other hands.

In the judgment of not a few who have given study and reflection to this matter, the nation has outgrown the provisions which the Constitution has established for filling the minor offices in the public service.

But whatever may be thought of the wisdom or expediency of changing the fundamental law in this regard, it is certain that much relief may be afforded, not only to the President and to the heads of the Departments, but to Senators and Representatives in Congress, by discreet legislation. They would be protected in a great measure by the bill now pending before the Senate, or by any other which should embody its important features, from the pressure of personal importunity and from the labor of examining conflicting claims and pretensions of candidates.

I trust that before the close of the present session some decisive action may be taken for the correction of the evils which inhere in the present methods of appointment, and I assure you of my hearty co-operation in any measures which are likely to conduce to that end.

As to the most appropriate term and tenure of the official life of the subordinate employés of the Government, it seems to be generally agreed that, whatever their extent or character, the one should be definite and the other stable, and that neither should be regulated by zeal in the service of party or fidelity to the fortunes of an individual.

It matters little to the people at large what competent person is at the head of this Department or of that Bureau, if they feel assured that the removal of one and the accession of another will not involve the retirement of honest and faithful subordinates, whose duties are purely administrative and have no legitimate connection with the triumph of any political principles or the success of any political party or faction. It is to this latter class of officers that the Senate bill, to which I have already referred, exclusively applies.

While neither that bill nor any other prominent scheme for improving the civil service concerns the higher grade of officials, who are appointed by the President and confirmed by the Senate, I feel bound to correct a prevalent misapprehension as to the frequency with which the present Executive has displaced the incumbent of an office and appointed another in his stead.

It has been repeatedly alleged that he has in this particular signally departed from the course which has been pursued under recent administrations of the Government. The facts are as follows:

The whole number of Executive appointments during the four years immediately preceding Mr. Garfield's accession to the Presidency was 2,696.

Of this number 244, or 9 per cent., involved the removal of previous incumbents.

The ratio of removals to the whole number of appointments was much the same during each of those four years.

In the first year, with 790 appointments, there were 74 removals, or 9.3 per cent.; in the second, with 917 appointments, there were 85 removals, or 8.5 per cent.; in the third, with 480 appointments, there were 48 removals, or 10 per cent.; in the fourth, with 429 appointments, there were 37 removals, or 8.6 per cent. In the four months of President Garfield's administration there were 390 appointments and 89 removals, or 22.7 per cent. Precisely the same number of removals (89) has taken place in the fourteen months which have since elapsed, but they constitute only 7.8 per cent. of the whole number of appointments (1,118) within that period, and less than 2.6 of the entire list of officials (3,459), exclusive of the Army and Navy, which is filled by Presidential appointment.

I declare my approval of such legislation as may be found necessary for supplementing the existing provisions of law in relation to political assessments.

In July last I authorized a public announcement that employés of the Government should regard themselves as at liberty to exercise their pleasure in making or refusing to make political contributions, and that their action in that regard would in no manner affect their official status.

In this announcement I acted upon the view which I had always maintained and still maintain, that a public officer should be as absolutely free as any other citizen to give or to withhold a contribution for the aid of the political party of his choice. It has, however, been urged, and doubtless not without foundation in fact, that by solicitation of official superiors and by other modes such contributions have at times been obtained from persons whose only motive for giving has been the fear of what might befall them if they refused. It goes without saying that such contributions are not voluntary, and in my judgment their collection should be prohibited by law. A bill which will effectually suppress them will receive my cordial approval.

I hope that however numerous and urgent may be the demands upon your attention, the interests of this District will not be forgotten.

The denial to its residents of the great right of suffrage in all its relation to national, State, and municipal action imposes upon Congress the duty of affording them the best administration which its wisdom can devise.

The report of the District Commissioners indicates certain measures whose adoption would seem to be very desirable. I instance in particular those which relate to arrears of taxes, to steam railroads, and to assessments of real property.

Among the questions which have been the topic of recent debate in the halls of Congress none are of greater gravity than those relating to the ascertainment of the vote for Presidential electors and the intendment of the Constitution in its provisions for devolving Executive functions upon the Vice-President when the President suffers from inability to discharge the powers and duties of his office.

11*

I trust that no embarrassments may result from a failure to determine these questions before another national election.

The closing year has been replete with blessings for which we owe to the Giver of all Good our reverent acknowledgment. For the uninterrupted harmony of our foreign relations, for the decay of sectional animosities, for the exuberance of our harvests and the triumphs of our mining and manufacturing industries, for the prevalence of health, the spread of intelligence and the conservation of the public credit, for the growth of the country in all the elements of national greatness—for these and countless other blessings—we should rejoice and be glad. I trust that, under the inspiration of this great prosperity, our counsels may be harmonious, and that the dictates of prudence, patriotism, justice, and economy may lead to the adoption of measures in which the Congress and the Executive may heartily unite.

CHESTER A. ARTHUR.

WASHINGTON, *December 4, 1882.*

MESSAGE

CONCERNING THE

REFERENCE OF CERTAIN CLAIMS TO THE COURT OF CLAIMS,

JANUARY 26, 1883.

MESSAGE.

To the House of Representatives:

It is hereby announced to the house of Congress in which it originated that the joint resolution (H. Res. 190) "to refer certain claims to the Court of Claims" has been permitted to become a law under the constitutional provision.

Its apparent purpose is to allow certain bankers to sue in the Court of Claims for the amount of internal-revenue tax collected from them without lawful authority, upon showing as matter of excuse for not having brought their suits within the time limited by law that they had entered into an agreement with the district attorney, which was in substance that they should be relieved of that necessity.

I cannot concur in the policy of setting aside the bar of the statute in those cases on such ground, but I have not deemed it necessary to return the joint resolution with my objections for reconsideration.

CHESTER A. ARTHUR.

Executive Mansion, *January 26, 1883.*

MESSAGE

CONCERNING

COMMERCIAL RELATIONS BETWEEN THE UNITED STATES AND MEXICO,

FEBRUARY 3, 1883.

MESSAGE.

I transmit to the Senate for consideration, with a view to ratification, the treaty of commerce which was signed in duplicate January 20, 1883, by commissioners on the part of the United States and Mexico, with accompanying papers.

The attention of the Senate is called to the statement in the third protocol as to the insertion of the word "steel" in item No. (35) 66 of the list appended to article 2 of the treaty. No further information as to the possible correction therein referred to has yet reached me; but as the session of the Senate will soon terminate, I deem it advisable to transmit the treaty as signed, in the hope that its ratification may be assented to.

While the treaty does not contain all the provisions desired by the United States, the difficulties in the way of a full and complete settlement of matters of common interest to the two countries were such as to make me willing to approve it as an important step towards a desirable result, not doubting that, as time shall show the advantages of the system thus inaugurated, the Government will be able by supplementary agreements to insert the word "steel" and to perfect what is lacking in the instrument.

CHESTER A. ARTHUR.

Executive Mansion,
Washington, February 3, 1883.

MESSAGE

NOMINATING A

CHIEF EXAMINER OF THE CIVIL SERVICE COMMISSION,

MARCH 1, 1883.

MESSAGE.

To the Senate of the United States:

To the Senate of the United States:

Having approved the act recently passed by Congress "to regulate and improve the civil service of the United States," I deem it my duty to call your attention to the provision for the employment of a "chief examiner" contained in the third section of the act, which was the subject of consideration at the time of its approval.

I am advised by the Attorney-General that there is great doubt whether such examiner is not properly an officer of the United States because of the nature of his employment, its duration, emolument, and duties. If he be such, the provision for his employment (which involves an appointment by the Commission) is not in conformity with section 2, article 2 of the Constitution. Assuming this to be the case, the result would be that the appointment of the chief examiner must be deemed to be vested in the President, by and with the advice and consent of the Senate, since in such case the appointment would not be otherwise provided for by law. Concurring in this opinion, I nominate Silas W. Burt, of New York, to be chief examiner of the Civil Service Commission.

CHESTER A. ARTHUR.

EXECUTIVE MANSION, *March 1, 1883.*

LETTER

CONCERNING

THE SOUTHERN EXPOSITION AT LOUISVILLE,

JUNE 9, 1883.

175

LETTER.

EXECUTIVE MANSION,
Washington, June 9, 1883.

MY DEAR SIR: I trust that my delay in answering your communication touching the proposed Southern Exposition at Louisville in August next has not been misinterpreted. It is in nowise attributable to lack of interest in the great undertaking to which you have invited my attention. That undertaking, on the contrary, richly deserves approval. It commands and will receive my personal and efficient encouragement. It seems to me, indeed, that its importance to the whole country, and especially to the South, can scarcely be overestimated.

Such exhibitions have come to be among the most marked features and the most instructive agents of our modern civilization; for they enhance the dignity of labor, and show to both labor and capital how inextricably their interests are interwoven. They elevate the standard of industrial attainment and give fresh and enduring impetus to inventive genius and skill. No time was ever more auspicious than the present for such an enterprise nor could it find a home in any more fitting spot than that which has been chosen for it. You are not misled by enthusiasm; you but speak "the words of truth and soberness" when you say that the South has entered upon a new era, in which, as I believe, it is destined to display, in the development of its marvelous resources, such zeal and energy as have never yet been exhibited in any region of our country at any period of our national life.

The proposed exhibition will disclose how vast a field the South now offers for every phase of industrial effort, in the mine, the field, the factory, everywhere, indeed, where art and skill can find room for employment; and the influences of this noble undertaking will

12*

ADDRESS

DELIVERED AT THE

OPENING OF THE SOUTHERN EXPOSITION AT LOUISVILLE

AUGUST 2, 1883.

ADDRESS.

I count myself fortunate that I am within the borders of this beautiful city of the South on a day which must be henceforth famous in its history. For a great undertaking, an undertaking of national interest and importance, enters here and now upon its career. I congratulate the promoters and managers of this Exposition that, even at the very threshold of its existence it gives abundant pledges of success. The zeal and enthusiasm which they have displayed in their labors of preparation; the frequent tidings of encouragement and cheer by which those labors have been lightened and made glad; the splendid triumphs of American genius, activity, and skill that are arrayed within these walls; the presence of the eager multitudes who throng these hospitable streets; all are tokens that the enterprise here inaugurated will be crowned with brilliant, far-reaching, enduring results.

It will multiply the aims of industry, better its operations, and elevate its standard of attainment. By suggesting new wants it will incite new activities. It will disclose natural resources as yet almost unexplored, and point the way to their prompt and profitable development. In countless ways it will promote the arts of peace and help to bring about the works of peace, proclaiming harmony and good-will and brotherly kindness throughout all the land unto all the inhabitants thereof.

I now declare that the Southern Exposition is open, and may God speed the fulfillment of all its lofty and ennobling purposes!

PROCLAMATION

THE WORLD'S INDUSTRIAL AND COTTON CENTENNIAL EXPOSITION AT NEW ORLEANS,

SEPTEMBER 10, 1883.

PROCLAMATION.

A PROCLAMATION.

Whereas by the eighth section of an act entitled "An act to encourage the holding of a World's Industrial and Cotton Centennial Exposition in the year eighteen hundred and eighty-four," approved February 10, 1883, it was enacted as follows:

"That whenever the President shall be informed by the said board of management that provision has been made for suitable buildings, or the erection of the same, for the purposes of said exhibition, the President shall, through the Department of State, make proclamation of the same, setting forth the time at which the exhibition will open and the place at which it will be held, and such board of management shall communicate to the diplomatic representatives of all nations copies of the same and a copy of this act together with such regulations as may be adopted by said board of management for publication in their respective countries."

And whereas the duly constituted board of managers of the aforesaid World's Industrial and Cotton Centennial Exposition has informed me that provision has been made for the erection of suitable buildings for the purposes of said Exposition:

Now, therefore, I, CHESTER A. ARTHUR, President of the United States of America, by authority of and in fulfillment of the requirements of said act approved February 10, 1883, do hereby declare and make known that the World's Industrial and Cotton Centennial Exposition will be opened on the first Monday in December, 1884, at the city of New Orleans, in the State of Louisiana, and will there be holden continuously until the 31st day of May, 1885.

ADDRESS

AT THE

UNVEILING OF THE BURNSIDE MONUMENT,

BRISTOL, RHODE ISLAND, SEPTEMBER 25, 1883.

ADDRESS.

I heartily join with you in paying tribute to the memory of that distinguished citizen of Rhode Island whose name yonder structure is henceforth privileged to bear. So long as it shall endure it will, in some degree, serve to perpetuate the fame of a soldier faithful to his trusts, whose courage found its only rival in his modesty; of a statesman whose every act was prompted by the loftiest patriotism, and of an earnest, sincere, and manly gentleman who abounded in all courtesy, who scorned all deceit, and who never failed to follow in the path of duty whithersoever it led.

PROCLAMATION

THURSDAY, NOVEMBER 29, 1883, AS A DAY OF NATIONAL THANKSGIVING.

OCTOBER 26, 1883.

191

PROCLAMATION.

A PROCLAMATION.

In furtherance of the custom of this people at the closing of each year to engage, upon a day set apart for that purpose, in a special festival of praise to the Giver of all good, I, CHESTER A. ARTHUR, President of the United States, do hereby designate Thursday, the twenty-ninth day of November next, as a day of national thanksgiving.

The year which is drawing to an end has been replete with evidences of Divine goodness.

The prevalence of health, the fulness of the harvests, the stability of peace and order, the growth of fraternal feeling, the spread of intelligence and learning, the continued enjoyment of civil and religious liberty—all these and countless other blessings are cause for reverent rejoicing.

I do therefore recommend that on the day above appointed the people rest from their accustomed labors, and meeting in their several places of worship, express their devout gratitude to God that He hath dealt so bountifully with this nation and pray that His grace and favor abide with it forever.

In witness whereof I have hereunto set my hand and caused the seal of the United States to be affixed. Done at the city of Washington this 26th day of October, in the year of our Lord one thousand eight hundred and eighty-three, and of the Independence of the United States the one hundred and eighth.

[SEAL.] CHESTER A. ARTHUR.

By the President:

FRED'K T. FRELINGHUYSEN,
Secretary of State.

ÁDDRESS

UNVEILING OF THE STATUE TO WASHINGTON ON THE STEPS OF THE TREASURY IN NEW YORK CITY,

NOVEMBER 26, 1883.

ADDRESS.

The President said:

Mr. President and fellow-citizens, it is fitting that other lips than mine should give voice to the sentiments of pride and patriotism which this occasion cannot fail to inspire in every heart. To myself has been assigned but a slight and formal part in the day's exercises, and I shall not exceed its becoming limits. I have come to this historic spot where the first President of the Republic took oath to preserve, protect, and defend its Constitution, simply to accept in behalf of the Government this tribute to his memory. Long may the noble statue you have here set up stand where you have placed it, a monument alike to your own generosity and public spirit, and to the wisdom and virtue and genius of the immortal Washington!

197

MESSAGE

TO THE

SENATE AND HOUSE OF REPRESENTATIVES,

DECEMBER 4, 1883.

MESSAGE

TO THE

·SENATE AND HOUSE OF REPRESENTATIVES,

DECEMBER 4, 1883.

MESSAGE.

To the Congress of the United States:

At the threshold of your deliberations I congratulate you upon the favorable aspect of the domestic and foreign affairs of this Government.

Our relations with other countries continue to be upon a friendly footing.

With the Argentine Republic, Austria, Belgium, Brazil, Denmark, Hayti, Italy, Santo Domingo, and Sweden and Norway no incident has occurred which calls for special comment. The recent opening of new lines of telegraphic communication with Central America and Brazil permitted the interchange of messages of friendship with the Governments of those countries.

During the year there have been perfected and proclaimed consular and commercial treaties with Serbia and a consular treaty with Roumania, thus extending our intercourse with the Danubian countries, while our Eastern relations have been put upon a wider basis by treaties with Corea and Madagascar. The new boundary-survey treaty with Mexico, a trades-mark convention and a supplementary treaty of extradition with Spain, and conventions extending the duration of the Franco-American Claims Commission have also been proclaimed.

Notice of the termination of the fisheries articles of the Treaty of Washington was duly given to the British Government, and the reciprocal privileges and exemptions of the treaty will accordingly cease on July 1, 1885. The fisheries industries, pursued by a numerous class of our citizens on the northern coasts, both of the Atlantic and Pacific Oceans, are worthy of the fostering care of Congress. Whenever brought into competition with the like in-

dustries of other countries, our fishermen, as well as our manufacturers of fishing appliances and preparers of fish products, have
maintained a foremost place. I suggest that Congress create a
commission to consider the general question of our rights in the
fisheries and the means of opening to our citizens, under just and
enduring conditions, the richly stocked fishing waters and sealing
grounds of British North America.

Question has arisen touching the deportation to the United States
from the British Islands, by governmental or municipal aid, of persons unable there to gain a living and equally a burden on the community here. Such of these persons as fall under the pauper class
as defined by law have been sent back in accordance with the provisions of our statutes. Her Majesty's Government has insisted that
precautions have been taken before shipment to prevent these objectionable visitors from coming hither without guarantee of support
by their relatives in this country. The action of the British authorities in applying measures for relief has, however, in so many cases
proved ineffectual, and especially so in certain recent instances of
needy emigrants reaching our territory through Canada, that a
revision of our legislation upon this subject may be deemed advisable.
Correspondence relative to the Clayton-Bulwer Treaty has been continued and will be laid before Congress.

The legislation of France against the importation of prepared
swine products from the United States has been repealed. That
result is due no less to the friendly representations of this Government than to a growing conviction in France that the restriction
was not demanded by any real danger to health.

Germany still prohibits the introduction of all swine products
from America. I extended to the Imperial Government a friendly
invitation to send experts to the United States to inquire whether
the use of those products was dangerous to health. This invitation
was declined. I have believed it of such importance however that
the exact facts should be ascertained and promulgated that I have
appointed a competent commission to make a thorough investigation of the subject. Its members have shown their public spirit by

accepting their trust without pledge of compensation, but I trust that Congress will see in the national and international bearings of the matter a sufficient motive for providing at least for reimbursement of such expenses as they may necessarily incur.

The coronation of the Czar at Moscow afforded to tnis Government an occasion for testifying its continued friendship by sending a special envoy and a representative of the Navy to attend the ceremony.

While there have arisen during the year no grave questions affecting the status in the Russian Empire of American citizens of other faith than that held by the national church, this Government remains firm in its conviction thàt the rights of its citizens abroad should be in no wise affected by their religious belief.

It is understood that measures for the removal of the restrictions which now burden our trade with Cuba and Puerto Rico are under consideration by the Spanish Government.

The proximity of Cuba to the United States and the peculiar methods of administration which there prevail necessitate constant discussion and appeal on our part from the proceedings of the insular authorities. I regret to say that the just protests of this Government have not as yet produced satisfactory results.

The commission appointed to decide certain claims of our citizens against the Spanish Government, after the recognition of a satisfactory rule as to the validity and force of naturalization in the United States, has finally adjourned. Some of its awards, though made more than two years ago, have not yet been paid. Their speedy payment is expected.

Claims to a large amount which were held by the late commission to be without its jurisdiction have been diplomatically presented to the Spanish Government. As the action of the colonial authorities, which has given rise to these claims, was admittedly illegal, full reparation for the injury sustained by our citizens shouldbe no longer delayed.

The case of the Masonic has not yet reached a settlement. The Manila court has found that the proceedings of which this Government has complained were unauthorized, and it is hoped that the

Government of Spain will not withhold the speedy reparation which its sense of justice should impel it to offer for the unusual severity and unjust action of its subordinate colonial officers in the case of this vessel.

The Helvetian Confederation has proposed the inauguration of a class of international treaties for the referment to arbitration of grave questions between nations. This Government has assented to the proposed negotiation of such a treaty with Switzerland.

Under the Treaty of Berlin, liberty of conscience and civil rights are assured to all strangers in Bulgaria. As the United States have no distinct conventional relations with that country and are not a party to the treaty, they should in my opinion maintain diplomatic representation at Sofia for the improvement of intercourse and the proper protection of the many American citizens who resort to that country as missionaries and teachers. I suggest that I be given authority to establish an agency and consulate-general at the Bulgarian capital.

The United States are now participating in a revision of the tariffs of the Ottoman Empire. They have assented to the application of a license tax to foreigners doing business in Turkey but have opposed the oppressive storage tax upon petroleum entering the ports of that country.

The Government of the Khedive has proposed that the authority of the mixed-judicial tribunals in Egypt be extended so as to cover citizens of the United States accused of crime, who are now triable before consular courts. This Government is not indisposed to accept the change, but believes that its terms should be submitted for criticism to the commission appointed to revise the whole subject.

At no time in our national history has there been more manifest need of close and lasting relations with a neighboring state than now exists with respect to Mexico. The rapid influx of our capital and enterprise into that country shows, by what has already been accomplished, the vast reciprocal advantages which must attend the progress of its internal development. The treaty of commerce and navigation of 1848 has been terminated by the Mexican Government, and in the absence of conventional engagements the rights of our citizens in Mexico now depend upon the domestic statutes of that Republic. There have been instances of harsh enforcement of the laws against our vessels and citizens in Mexico, and of denial of the diplomatic resort for their protection. The initial step toward a better understanding has been taken in the negotiation by the commission authorized by Congress of a treaty which is still before the Senate awaiting its approval.

The provisions for the reciprocal crossing of the frontier by the troops in pursuit of hostile Indians have been prolonged for another year. The operations of the forces of both Governments against these savages have been successful, and several of their most dangerous bands have been captured or dispersed by the skill and valor of United States and Mexican soldiers fighting in a common cause.

The convention for the resurvey of the boundary from the Rio Grande to the Pacific, having been ratified and exchanged, the preliminary reconnaissance therein stipulated has been effected. It now rests with Congress to make provision for completing the survey and relocating the boundary monuments.

A convention was signed with Mexico on July 13, 1882, providing for the rehearing of the cases of Benjamin Weil and the Abra Silver Mining Company, in whose favor awards were made by the late American and Mexican Claims Commission. That convention still awaits the consent of the Senate. Meanwhile because of those charges of fraudulent awards which have made a new commission necessary, the Executive has directed the suspension of payments of the distributive quota received from Mexico.

Our geographical proximity to Central America and our political and commercial relations with the states of that country justify, in my judgment, such a material increase of our consular corps as will place at each capital a consul-general.

The contest between Bolivia, Chile, and Peru has passed from the stage of strategic hostilities to that of negotiation, in which the counsels of this Government have been exercised. The demands of Chile for absolute cession of territory have been maintained and accepted by the party of General Iglesias to the extent of concluding a treaty of peace with the Government of Chile in general conformity with the terms of the protocol signed in May last between the Chilean commander and General Iglesias. As a result of the conclusion of this treaty, General Iglesias has been formally recognized by Chile as President of Peru, and his Government installed at Lima which has been evacuated by the Chileans. A call has been issued by General Iglesias for a representative assembly, to be elected on the 13th of January, and to meet at Lima on the 1st of March next. Meanwhile the provisional government of General Iglesias has applied for recognition to the principal powers of America and Europe. When the will of the Peruvian people shall be manifested I shall not hesitate to recognize the Government approved by them.

Diplomatic and naval representatives of this Government attended at Caracas the centennial celebration of the birth of the illustrious Bolivar. At the same time the inauguration of the statue of Washington in the Venezuelan capital testified to the veneration in which his memory is there held.

Congress at its last session authorized the Executive to propose to Venezuela a reopening of the awards of the Mixed Commission of Caracas. The departure from this country of the Venezuelan minister has delayed the opening of negotiations for reviving the commission. This Government holds that until the establishment of a treaty upon this subject the Venezuelan Government must continue to make the payments provided for in the convention of 1866.

There is ground for believing that the dispute growing out of the unpaid obligations due from Venezuela to France will be satisfactorily adjusted. The French cabinet has proposed a basis of settlement which meets my approval, but as it involves a recasting of the annual quotas of the foreign debt it has been deemed advisable to submit the proposal to the judgment of the cabinets of Berlin, Copenhagen, The Hague, London, and Madrid.

At the recent coronation of His Majesty King Kalakaua this Government was represented both diplomatically and by the formal visit of a vessel of war.

The question of terminating or modifying the existing reciprocity treaty with Hawaii is now before Congress. I am convinced that the charges of abuses and frauds under that treaty have been exaggerated, and I renew the suggestion of last year's message that the treaty be modified wherever its provisions have proved onerous to legitimate trade between the two countries. I am not disposed to favor the entire cessation of the treaty relations which have fostered good-will between the countries and contributed toward the equality of Hawaii in the family of nations.

In pursuance of the policy declared by this Government of extending our intercourse with the Eastern nations, legations have during the past year been established in Persia, Siam, and Corea. It is probable that permanent missions of those countries will ere long be maintained in the United States. A special embassy from Siam is now on its way hither.

Treaty relations with Corea were perfected by the exchange at Seôul, on the 19th of May last, of the ratifications of the lately concluded convention, and envoys from the King of Tah Chosun have visited this country and received a cordial welcome. Corea, as yet unacquainted with the methods of Western civilization, now invites the attention of those interested in the advancement of our foreign trade, as it needs the implements and products which the United States are ready to supply. We seek no monopoly of its commerce and no advantages over other nations, but as the Chosunese, in reaching for a higher civilization, have confided in this Republic, we cannot regard with indifference any encroachment on their rights.

China, by the payment of a money indemnity, has settled certain of the long-pending claims of our citizens, and I have strong hopes that the remainder will soon be adjusted.

Questions have arisen touching the rights of American and other foreign manufacturers in China under the provisions of treaties which permit aliens to exercise their industries in that country. On this specific point our own treaty is silent, but under the operation of the most-favored-nation clause, we have like privileges with those of other powers. While it is the duty of the Government to see that our citizens have the full enjoyment of every benefit secured by treaty, I doubt the expediency of leading in a movement to constrain China to admit an interpretation which we have only an indirect treaty right to exact. The transference to China of American capital for the employment there of Chinese labor would in effect inaugurate a competition for the control of markets now supplied by our home industries.

There is good reason to believe that the law restricting the immigration of Chinese has been violated, intentionally or otherwise, by the officials of China upon whom is devolved the duty of certifying that the immigrants belong to the excepted classes.

Measures have been taken to ascertain the facts incident to this supposed infraction, and it is believed that the Government of China will co-operate with the United States in securing the faithful observance of the law.

The same considerations which prompted Congress at its last session to return to Japan the Simonoseki indemnity seem to me to require at its hands like action in respect to the Canton indemnity fund, now amounting to $300,000.

The question of the general revision of the foreign treaties of Japan has been considered in an international conference held at Tokio, but without definite result as yet. This Government is disposed to concede the requests of Japan to determine its own tariff duties, to provide such proper judicial tribunals as may commend themselves to the Western Powers for the trial of causes to which foreigners are parties, and to assimilate the terms and duration of its treaties to those of other civilized States.

Through our ministers at London and at Monrovia, this Government has endeavored to aid Liberia in its differences with Great Britain touching the northwestern boundary of that republic. There is a prospect of adjustment of the dispute by the adoption of the Mannah River as the line. This arrangement is a compromise of the conflicting territorial claims, and takes from Liberia no country over which it has maintained effective jurisdiction.

The rich and populous valley of the Congo is being opened to commerce by a society called the International African Association, of which the King of the Belgians is the president and a citizen of the United States the chief executive officer. Large tracts of territory have been ceded to the association by native chiefs, roads have been opened, steamboats placed on the river, and the *nuclei* of states established at twenty-two stations under one flag which offers freedom to commerce and prohibits the slave trade. The objects of the society are philanthropic. It does not aim at permanent political control but seeks the neutrality of the valley. The United States cannot be indifferent to this work nor to the interests of their citizens involved in it. It may become advisable for us to co-operate with other commercial powers in promoting the rights of trade and residence in the Congo Valley free from the interference or political control of any one nation.

In view of the frequency of invitations from foreign Governments to participate in social and scientific congresses for the discussion of important matters of general concern, I repeat the suggestion of my last message, that provision be made for the exercise of discretionary power by the Executive in appointing delegates to such convocations. Able specialists are ready to serve the national interests in such capacity without personal profit or other compensation than the defrayment of expenses actually incurred, and this a comparatively small annual appropriation would suffice to meet.

I have alluded in my previous messages to the injurious and vexatious restrictions suffered by our trade in the Spanish West Indies. Brazil, whose natural outlet for its great national staple, coffee, is in and through the United States, imposes a heavy export duty upon that product. Our petroleum exports are hampered in Turkey and in other Eastern ports by restrictions as to storage and by onerous taxation. For these mischiefs adequate relief is not always afforded by reciprocity treaties like that with Hawaii or that lately negotiated with Mexico and now awaiting the action of the Senate. Is it not advisable to provide some measure of equitable retaliation in our relations with Governments which discriminate against our own? If, for example, the Executive were empowered to apply to Spanish vessels and cargoes from Cuba and Puerto Rico the same rules of treatment and scale of penalties for technical faults which are applied to our

14*

vessels and cargoes in the Antilles, a resort to that course might not
be barren of good results.

The report of the Secretary of the Treasury gives a full and interesting exhibit of the financial condition of the country.
It shows that the ordinary revenues from all
   sources for the fiscal year ended June 30, 1883,
   amounted to $398,287,581 95
Whereof there was received—

From customs......................	$214,706,496 93	
From internal revenue	144,720,368 98	
From sales of public lands...	7,955,864 42	
From tax on circulation and deposits of national banks..	9,111,008 85	
From profits on coinage, bullion deposits, and assays	4,460,205 17	
From other sources..............	17,333,637 60	
Total		398,287,581 95

For the same period the ordinary expenditures
   were:

For civil expenses.........	$22,343,285 76
For foreign intercourse..........	2,419,275 24
For Indians..............	7,362,590 34
For pensions	66,012,573 64
For the military establishment, including river and harbor improvements and arsenals.........	48,911,382 93
For the naval establishment, including vessels, machinery, and improvements at navy-yards..	15,283,437 17
For miscellaneous expenditures, including public buildings, light-houses, and collecting the revenue	40,098,432 73
For expenditures on account of the District of Columbia	3,817,028 48
For interest on the public debt	59,160,131 25
Total	265,408,137 54

Leaving a surplus revenue of............................	$132,879,444 41
Which, with an amount drawn from the cash balance in the Treasury of	1,299,312 55
Making................................	134,178,756 96

Was applied to the redemption—

Of bonds for the sinking-fund........	44,850,700 00
Of fractional currency for the sinking-fund......	46,556 96
Of funded loan of 1881, continued at 3½ per cent	65,380,250 00
Of loan of July and August, 1861, continued at 3½ per cent	20,594,600 00
Of funded loan of 1907..............................	1,418,850 00
Of funded loan of 1881...............................	719,150 00
Of loan of February, 1861	18,000 00
Of loan of July and August, 1861	266,600 00
Of loan of March, 1863	116,850 00
Of loan of July, 1882	47,650 00
Of five-twenties of 1862	10,300 00
Of five-twenties of 1864	7,050 00
Of five-twenties of 1865..............................	9,600 00
Of ten-forties of 1864	133,550 00
Of consols of 1865...................................	40,800 00
Of consols of 1867......................	235,700 00
Of consols of 1868........................	154,650 00
Of Oregon-war debt	5,450 00
Of refunding certificates	109,150 00
Of old demand, compound-interest, and other notes	13,300 00
Total	134,178,756 96

The revenue for the present fiscal year, actual and estimated, is as follows:

Source.	For the quarter ended September 30, 1883. Actual.	For the remaining three quarters of the year. Estimated.
From customs	$57,402,975 67	$137,597,004 33
From internal revenue..........	29,662,078 60	90,337,921 40
From sales of public lands....	2,932,635 17	5,067,364 83
From tax on circulation and deposits of national banks	1,557,800 88	1,542,199 12
From repayment of interest and sinking-fund, Pacific railway companies	521,059 51	1,478,940 49
From customs fees, fines, penalties, &c	298,696 78	901,303 22
From fees—consular, letters-patent, and lands..........	863,209 80	2,436,790 20
From proceeds of sales of Government property..........	112,562 23	167,437 77
From profits on coinage, &c	950,229 46	3,149,770 54
From deposits for surveying public lands	172,461 31	327,538 69
From revenues of the District of Columbia..........	256,017 99	1,643,982 01
From miscellaneous sources	1,937,189 63	2,382,810 37
Total receipts...	95,966,917 03	247,033,082 97

The actual and estimated expenses for the same period are:

Object.	For the quarter ended September 30, 1883. Actual.	For the remaining three quarters of the year. Estimated.
For civil and miscellaneous expenses, including public buildings, light-houses, and collecting the revenue	$15,385,799 42	$51,114,200 58
For Indians	2,623,390 54	4,126,609 46
For pensions.	16,285,261 98	53,714,738 02
For military establishment, including fortifications, river and harbor improvements, and arsenals..........	13,512,204 33	26,487,795 67
For naval establishment, including vessels and machinery, and improvements at navy-yards	4,190,299 69	12,300,700 31
For expenditures on account of the District of Columbia.	1,138,836 41	2,611,163 59
For interest on the public debt.......	14,797,297 96	39,702,702 04
Total ordinary expenditures	67,942,090 33	190,057,909 67

Total receipts, actual and estimated $343,000,000 00

Total expenditures, actual and estimated..........   258,000,000 00

        85,000,000 00

Estimated amount due the sinking-fund 45,816,741 07

Leaving a balance of.......... ....   39,183,258 93

If the revenue for the fiscal year which will end on June 30, 1885, be estimated upon the basis of existing laws, the Secretary is of the opinion that for that year the receipts will exceed by $60,000,000 the ordinary expenditures including the amount devoted to the sinking-fund.

Hitherto the surplus as rapidly as it has accumulated has been devoted to the reduction of the national debt.

As a result the only bonds now outstanding which are redeemable at the pleasure of the Government are the three per cents, amounting to about $305,000,000.

The four and one-half per cents, amounting to $250,000,000, and the $737,000,000 four per cents are not payable until 1891 and 1907, respectively.

If the surplus shall hereafter be as large as the Treasury estimates now indicate, the three per cent. bonds may all be redeemed at least four years before any of the four and one-half per cents can be called in. The latter at the same rate of accumulation of surplus can be paid at maturity and the moneys requisite for the redemption of the four per cents will be in the Treasury many years before those obligations become payable.

There are cogent reasons however why the national indebtedness should not be thus rapidly extinguished. Chief among them is the fact that only by excessive taxation is such rapidity attainable.

In a communication to the Congress at its last session I recommended that all excise taxes be abolished except those relating to distilled spirits and that substantial reductions be also made in the revenues from customs. A statute has since been enacted by which the annual tax and tariff receipts of the Government have been cut down to the extent of at least fifty or sixty millions of dollars.

While I have no doubt that still further reductions may be wisely made I do not advise the adoption at this session of any measures for large diminution of the national revenues. The results of the legislation of the last session of the Congress have not as yet become sufficiently apparent to justify any radical revision or sweeping modifications of existing law.

In the interval which must elapse before the effects of the act of March 3, 1883, can be definitely ascertained a portion at least of the surplus revenues may be wisely applied to the long-neglected duty of rehabilitating our Navy and providing coast defenses for the protection of our harbors. This is a matter to which I shall again advert.

Immediately associated with the financial subject just discussed is the important question what legislation is needed regarding the national currency.

The aggregate amount of bonds now on deposit in the Treasury to support the national-bank circulation is about $350,000,000. Nearly $200,000,000 of ·this amount consists of three per cents, which, as already stated, are payable at the pleasure of the Government and are likely to be called in within less than four years unless meantime the surplus revenues shall be diminished.

The probable effect of such an extensive retirement of the securities which are the basis of the national-bank circulation would be such a contraction of the volume of the currency as to produce grave commercial embarrassments.

How can this danger be obviated? The most effectual plan, and one whose adoption at the earliest practicable opportunity I shall heartily approve, has already been indicated.

If the revenues of the next four years shall be kept substantially commensurate with the expenses, the volume of circulation will not be likely to suffer any material disturbance.

But if, on the other hand, there shall be great delay in reducing taxation, it will become necessary either to substitute some other form of currency in place of the national-bank notes or to make important changes in the laws by which their circulation is now controlled.

In my judgment the latter course is far preferable. I commend to your attention the very interesting and thoughtful suggestions upon this subject which appear in the Secretary's report.

The objections which he urges against the acceptance of any other securities than the obligations of the Government itself as a foundation for national-bank circulation seem to me insuperable.

For averting the threatened contraction two courses have been suggested, either of which is probably feasible. One is the issuance of new bonds, having many years to run, bearing a low rate of interest, and exchangeable upon specified terms for those now outstanding. The other course, which commends itself to my own judgment as the better, is the enactment of a law repealing the tax on circulation and permitting the banks to issue notes for an amount equal to 90 per cent. of the market value instead of as now the face value of their deposited bonds. I agree with the Secretary in the belief that the adoption of this plan would afford the necessary relief.

The trade-dollar was coined for the purpose of traffic in countries where silver passed at its value as ascertained by its weight and fineness. It never had a legal-tender quality. Large numbers of these coins entered, however, into the volume of our currency. By common consent their circulation in domestic trade has now ceased, and they have thus become a disturbing element. They should not be longer permitted to embarrass our currency system. I recommend that provision be made for their reception by the Treasury and the mints, as bullion, at a small percentage above the current market price of silver of like fineness.

The Secretary of the Treasury advises a consolidation of certain of the customs districts of the country, and suggests that the President be vested with such power in relation thereto as is now given him in respect to collectors of internal revenue by section 3141 of the Revised Statutes. The statistics upon this subject which are contained in his report furnish of themselves a strong argument in defense of his views.

At the adjournment of Congress the number of internal-revenue collection districts was 126. By Executive order dated June 25, 1883, I directed that certain of these districts be consolidated. The result has been a reduction of one-third their number, which at present is but 83.

From the report of the Secretary of War it will be seen that in only a single instance has there been any disturbance of the quiet condition of our Indian tribes. A raid from Mexico into Arizona was made in March last by a small party of Indians, which was pursued by General Crook into the mountain regions from which it had come. It is confidently hoped that serious outbreaks will not again occur and that the Indian tribes which have for so many years disturbed the West will hereafter remain in peaceable submission.

I again call your attention to the present condition of our extended seacoast, upon which are so many large cities whose wealth and importance to the country would in time of war invite attack from modern armored ships against which our existing defensive works could give no adequate protection. Those works were built before the introduction of modern heavy rifled guns into maritime warfare, and if they are not put in an efficient condition we may easily be subjected to humiliation by a hostile power greatly inferior to ourselves. As germane to this subject, I call your attention to the importance of perfecting our submarine-torpedo defenses. The board authorized by the last Congress to report upon the method which should be adopted for the manufacture of heavy ordnance adapted to modern warfare has visited the principal iron and steel works in this country and in Europe. It is hoped that its report will soon be made, and that Congress will thereupon be disposed to provide suitable facilities and plant for the manufacture of such guns as are now imperatively needed.

On several occasions during the past year officers of the Army have at the request of the State authorities visited their militia encampments for inspection of the troops. From the reports of these officers I am induced to believe that the encouragement of the State militia organizations by the National Government would be followed by very gratifying results, and would afford it in sudden emergencies the aid of a large body of volunteers educated in the performance of military duties.

The Secretary of the Navy reports that under the authority of the acts of August 5, 1882, and March 3, 1883, the work of strengthening our Navy by the construction of modern vessels has been auspiciously begun. Three cruisers are in process of construction—the Chicago, of 4,500 tons displacement, and the Boston and Atlanta, each of 2,500 tons. They are to be built of steel, with the tensile strength and ductility prescribed by law, and in the combination of speed, endurance, and armament are expected to compare favorably with the best unarmored war vessels of other nations. A fourth vessel, the Dolphin, is to be constructed of similar material and is intended to serve as a fleet dispatch boat.

The double-turreted monitors Puritan, Amphitrite, and Terror have been launched on the Delaware River and a contract has been made for the supply of their machinery. A similar monitor, the Monadnock, has been launched in California.

The Naval Advisory Board and the Secretary recommend the completion of the monitors, the construction of four gunboats, and also of three additional steel vessels like the Chicago, Boston, and Dolphin.

As an important measure of national defense the Secretary urges also the immediate creation of an interior coast-line of water-ways across the Peninsula of Florida, along the coast from Florida to Hampton Roads, between the Chesapeake Bay and the Delaware River, and through Cape Cod.

I feel bound to impress upon the attention of Congress the necessity of continued progress in the reconstruction of the Navy. The condition of the public treasury, as I have already intimated, makes the present an auspicious time for putting this branch of the service in a state of efficiency.

It is no part of our policy to create and maintain a Navy able to cope with that of the other great powers of the world.

We have no wish for foreign conquest, and the peace which we have long enjoyed is in no seeming danger of interruption.

But that our naval strength should be made adequate for the defense of our harbors, the protection of our commercial interests, and the maintenance of our national honor, is a proposition from which no patriotic citizen can withhold his assent.

The report of the Postmaster-General contains a gratifying exhibit of the condition and prospects of the interesting branch of the public service committed to his care.

It appears that on June 30, 1883, the whole number of post-offices was 47,863, of which 1,632 were established during the previous fiscal year. The number of offices operating under the system of free delivery was 154.

At these latter offices the postage on local matter amounted to $4,195,230.52, a sum exceeding by $1,021,894.01 the entire cost of the carrier service of the country.

The rate of postage on drop letters passing through these offices is now fixed by law at two cents per half ounce or fraction thereof. In offices where the carrier system has not been established the rate is only half as large.

It will be remembered that in 1863, when free delivery was first established by law, the uniform single-rate postage upon local letters was one cent; and so it remained until 1872, when in those cities where carrier service was established it was increased in order to defray the expense of such service.

It seems to me that the old rate may now with propriety be restored, and that, too, even at the risk of diminishing for a time, at least, the receipts from postage upon local letters.

I can see no reason why that particular class of mail matter should be held accountable for the entire cost of not only its own collection and delivery but the collection and delivery of all other classes; and I am confident, after full consideration of the subject, that the reduction of rate would be followed by such a growing accession of business as to occasion but slight and temporary loss to the revenues of the Post-Office. The Postmaster-General devotes much of his report to the consideration, in its various aspects, of the relations of the Government to the telegraph. Such reflection as I have been able to give to this subject since my last annual message has not led me to change the views which I there expressed in dissenting from the recommendation of the then Postmaster-General that the Government assume the same control over the telegraph which it has always exercised over the mail.

Admitting that its authority in the premises is as ample as has ever been claimed for it, it would not, in my judgment, be a wise use of that authority to purchase or assume the control of existing telegraph lines, or to construct others with a view of entering into general competition with private enterprise.

The objections which may be justly urged against either of those projects, and indeed against any system which would require an enormous increase in the civil-service list, do not, however, apply to some of the plans which have lately provoked public comment and discussion. It has been claimed, for example, that Congress might wisely authorize the Postmaster-General to contract with some private persons or corporation for the transmission of messages, or of a certain class of messages, at specified rates and under Government supervision. Various such schemes, of the same general nature but widely differing in their special characteristics, have been suggested in the public prints, and the arguments by which they have been supported and opposed have doubtless attracted your attention.

It is likely that the whole subject will be considered by you at the present session.

In the nature of things it involves so many questions of detail that your deliberations would probably be aided slightly, if at all, by any particular suggestions which I might now submit.

I avow my belief, however, that the Government should be authorized by law to exercise some sort of supervision over interstate telegraphic communication, and I express the hope that for attaining that end some measure may be devised which will receive your approbation.

The Attorney-General criticises in his report the provisions of existing law fixing the fees of jurors and witnesses in the Federal courts. These provisions are chiefly contained in the act of February 26, 1853, though some of them were introduced into that act from statutes which had been passed many years previous. It is manifest that such compensation as might, when these laws were enacted, have been just and reasonable would in many instances be justly regarded at the present day as inadequate. I concur with the Attorney-General in the belief that the statutes should be revised by which these fees are regulated.

So, too, should the laws which regulate the compensation of district attorneys and marshals. They should be paid wholly by salaries, instead of in part by fees, as is now the case.

The change would prove to be a measure of economy, and would discourage the institution of needless and oppressive legal proceedings, which, it is to be feared, have in some instances been conducted for the mere sake of personal gain.

Much interesting and varied information is contained in the report of the Secretary of the Interior.

I particularly call your attention to his presentation of certain phases of the Indian question, to his recommendations for the repeal of the pre-emption and timber-culture acts, and for more stringent legislation to prevent frauds under the pension laws. The statutes which prescribe the definitions and punishments of crimes relating to pensions could doubtless be made more effective by certain amendments and additions which are pointed out in the Secretary's report.

I have previously referred to the alarming state of illiteracy in certain portions of the country, and again submit for the consideration of Congress whether some Federal aid should not be extended to public primary education wherever adequate provision therefor has not already been made.

The Utah Commission has submitted to the Secretary of the Interior its second annual report. As a result of its labors in supervising the recent election in that Territory, pursuant to the act of March 22, 1882, it appears that persons by that act disqualified, to the number of about 12,000, were excluded from the polls. This fact, however, affords little cause for congratulation, and I fear that it is far from indicating any real and substantial progress toward the extirpation of polygamy. All the members-elect of the legislature are Mormons. There is grave reason to believe that they are in sympathy with the practices that this Government is seeking to suppress, and that its efforts in that regard will be more likely to encounter their opposition than to receive their encouragement and support. Even if this view should happily be erroneous, the law under which the Commissioners have been acting should be made more effective by the incorporation of some such stringent amendments as they recommend, and as were included in bill No. 2238 on the Calendar of the Senate at its last session.

I am convinced, however, that polygamy has become so strongly intrenched in the Territory of Utah that it is profitless to attack it with any but the stoutest weapons which constitutional legislation can fashion. I favor therefore the repeal of the act upon which the existing government depends, the assumption by the national legislature of the entire political control of the Territory, and the establishment of a commission with such powers and duties as shall be delegated to it by law.

The Department of Agriculture is accomplishing much in the direction of the agricultural development of the country, and the report of the Commissioner giving the results of his investigations and experiments will be found interesting and valuable.

At his instance a convention of those interested in the cattle industry of the country was lately held at Chicago. The prevalence of pleuro-pneumonia and other contagious diseases of animals was one of the chief topics of discussion. A committee of the convention will invite your co-operation in investigating the causes of these diseases and providing methods for their prevention and cure.

I trust that Congress will not fail at its present session to put Alaska under the protection of law. Its people have repeatedly remonstrated against our neglect to afford them the maintenance and protection expressly guaranteed by the terms of the treaty whereby that Territory was ceded to the United States. For sixteen years they have pleaded in vain for that which they should have received without the asking.

They have no law for the collection of debts, the support of education, the conveyance of property, the administration of estates or the enforcement of contracts ; none indeed for the punishment of criminals except such as offend against certain customs, commerce and navigation acts.

The resources of Alaska, especially in fur, mines, and lumber, are considerable in extent and capable of large development, while its geographical situation is one of political and commercial importance.

The promptings of interest, therefore, as well as considerations of honor and good faith, demand the immediate establishment of civil government in that Territory.

Complaints have lately been numerous and urgent that certain corporations, controlling in whole or in part the facilities for the interstate carriage of persons and merchandise over the great railroads of the country, have resorted in their dealings with the public to divers measures unjust and oppressive in their character.

In some instances the State governments have attacked and suppressed these evils, but in others they have been unable to afford adequate relief because of the jurisdictional limitations which are imposed upon them by the Federal Constitution.

The question how far the National Government may lawfully interfere in the premises, and what, if any, supervision or control it ought to exercise, is one which merits your careful consideration.

While we cannot fail to recognize the importance of the vast railway systems of the country and their great and beneficent influences upon the development of our material wealth, we should, on the other hand, remember that no individual and no corporation ought to be invested with absolute power over the interest of any other citizen or class of citizens. The right of these railway corporations to a fair and profitable return upon their investments, and to reasonable freedom in their regulations, must be recognized; but it seems only just that, so far as its constitutional authority will permit, Congress should protect the people at large in their interstate traffic against acts of injustice which the State governments are powerless to prevent.

In my last annual message I called attention to the necessity of protecting by suitable legislation the forests situated upon the public domain. In many portions of the West the pursuit of general agriculture is only made practicable by resort to irrigation, while successful irrigation would itself be impossible without the aid afforded by forests in contributing to the regularity and constancy of the supply of water.

During the past year severe suffering and great loss of property have been occasioned by profuse floods followed by periods of unusually low water in many of the great rivers of the country.

These irregularities were in great measure caused by the removal from about the sources of the streams in question of the timber by which the water supply had been nourished and protected.

The preservation of such portions of the forests on the national domain as essentially contribute to the equable flow of important water-courses is of the highest consequence.

Important tributaries of the Missouri, the Columbia, and the Saskatchewan rise in the mountain region of Montana, near the northern boundary of the United States, between the Blackfeet and Flathead Indian reservations. This region is unsuitable for settlement, but upon the rivers which flow from it depends the future agricultural development of a vast tract of country. The attention of Congress is called to the necessity of withdrawing from public sale this part of the public domain and establishing there a forest preserve.

The industrial exhibitions which have been held in the United States during the present year attracted attention in many foreign countries where the announcement of those enterprises had been made public through the foreign agencies of this Government. The Industrial Exhibition at Boston and the Southern Exposition at Louisville were largely attended by the exhibitors of foreign countries, notwithstanding the absence of any professed national character in those undertakings.

The Centennial Exposition to be held next year at New Orleans, in commemoration of the centenary of the first shipment of cotton from a port of the United States bids fair to meet with like gratifying success. Under the act of Congress of the 10th of February, 1883, declaring that exposition to be national and international in its character, all foreign Governments with which the United States maintain relations have been invited to participate.

The promoters of this important undertaking have already received assurances of the lively interest which it has excited abroad.

The report of the Commissioners of the District of Columbia is herewith transmitted. I ask for it your careful attention, especially for those portions which relate to assessments, arrears of taxes, and increase of water supply.

The Commissioners who were appointed under the act of January 16, 1883, entitled "An act to regulate and improve the civil service of the United States," entered promptly upon the discharge of their duties.

A series of rules, framed in accordance with the spirit of the statute, was approved and promulgated by the President.

In some particulars wherein they seemed defective those rules were subsequently amended. It will be perceived that they discountenance any political or religious tests for admission to those offices of the public service to which the statute relates.

The act is limited in its original application to the classified clerkships in the several Executive Departments at Washington (numbering about 5,600) and to similar positions in customs districts and post-offices where as many as fifty persons are employed.

A classification of these positions analogous to that existing in the Washington offices was duly made before the law went into effect.

Eleven customs districts and twenty-three post-offices were thus brought under the immediate operation of the statute.

The annual report of the Civil Service Commission which will soon be submitted to Congress will doubtless afford the means of a more definite judgment than I am now prepared to express as to the merits of the new system. I am persuaded that its effects have thus far proved beneficial. Its practical methods appear to be adequate for the ends proposed, and there has been no serious difficulty in carrying them into effect. Since the 16th of July last no person, so far as I am aware, has been appointed to the public service in the classified portions thereof at any of the Departments, or at any of the post-offices and customs districts above named, except those certified by the Commission to be the most competent on the basis of the examinations held in conformity to the rules.

At the time when the present Executive entered upon his office his death, removal, resignation, or inability to discharge his duties would have left the Government without a constitutional head.

It is possible of course that a similar contingency may again arise unless the wisdom of Congress shall provide against its recurrence.

The Senate at its last session, after full consideration, passed an act relating to this subject which will now, I trust, commend itself to the approval of both houses of Congress.

The clause of the Constitution upon which must depend any law regulating the Presidential succession presents also for solution other questions of paramount importance.

These questions relate to the proper interpretation of the phrase "inability to discharge the powers and duties of said office," our organic law providing that, when the President shall suffer from such inability, the Presidential office shall devolve upon the Vice-

President, who must himself under like circumstances give place to such officer as Congress may by law appoint to act as President.

I need not here set forth the numerous and interesting inquiries which are suggested by these words of the Constitution. They were fully stated in my first communication to Congress and have since been the subject of frequent deliberations in that body.

It is greatly to be hoped that these momentous questions will find speedy solution, lest emergencies may arise when longer delay will be impossible, and any determination, albeit the wisest, may furnish cause for anxiety and alarm.

For the reasons fully stated in my last annual message I repeat my recommendation that Congress propose an amendment to that provision of the Constitution which prescribes the formalities for the enactment of laws, whereby, in respect to bills for the appropriation of public moneys, the Executive may be enabled, while giving his approval to particular items, to interpose his veto as to such others as do not commend themselves to his judgment.

The Fourteenth Amendment of the Constitution confers the rights of citizenship upon all persons born or naturalized in the United States and subject to the jurisdiction thereof. It was the special purpose of this amendment to insure to members of the colored race the full enjoyment of civil and political rights.

Certain statutory provisions intended to secure the enforcement of those rights have been recently declared unconstitutional by the Supreme Court.

Any legislation whereby Congress may lawfully supplement the guaranties which the Constitution affords for the equal enjoyment by all the citizens of the United States of every right, privilege, and immunity of citizenship will receive my unhesitating approval.

CHESTER A. ARTHUR.

WASHINGTON, *December 4, 1883.*

15*

PROCLAMATION

CONCERNING THE

COMMEMORATION OF THE ONE HUNDREDTH ANNIVERSARY OF THE SURRENDER, BY GEORGE WASHINGTON, OF HIS COMMISSION AS COMMANDER-IN-CHIEF OF THE PATRIOT FORCES OF AMERICA.

DECEMBER 21, 1883.

PROCLAMATION.

A PROCLAMATION.

Whereas both houses of Congress did, on the twentieth instant, request the commemoration on the twenty-third instant of the one hundredth anniversary of the surrender, by George Washington, at Annapolis, of his commission as commander-in-chief of the patriot forces of America; and

Whereas it is fitting that this memorable act, which not only signalized the termination of the heroic struggle of seven years for independence, but also manifested Washington's devotion to the great principle that ours is a civic Government of and by the people, should be generally observed throughout the United States:

Now, therefore, I, CHESTER A. ARTHUR, President of the United States, do hereby recommend that either by appropriate exercises in connection with the religious services of the twenty-third instant, or by such public observances as may be deemed proper on Monday, the twenty-fourth instant, this signal event in the history of American liberty be commemorated; and, further, I hereby direct that at 12 o'clock noon on Monday next the national salute be fired from all the forts throughout the country.

In witness whereof I have hereunto set my hand and caused the seal of the United States to be affixed.

Done this twenty-first day of December, in the year of our Lord one thousand eight hundred and eighty-three, and of the Independence of the United States the one hundred and eighth.

[SEAL.]   CHESTER A. ARTHUR.

By the President:

FRED'K T. FRELINGHUYSEN,
Secretary of State.

MESSAGE.

REPORT OF THE MISSISSIPPI RIVER COMMISSION.

JANUARY 8, 1884.

MESSAGE.

To the Senate and House of Representatives:

I transmit herewith to the House of Representatives a communication from the Secretary of War submitting the annual report of the Mississippi River Commission.

I take this occasion to invite the early attention of Congress to the continuation of the work on the Mississippi River, which is being carried on under the plans of the Commission. My sense of the importance of the improvement of this river, not only to the people of the Northwest, but especially to the inhabitants of the Lower Mississippi Valley, has already been expressed in a special communication to the last Congress. The harvests of grain and cotton produced in the region bordering upon the Mississippi are so vast as to be of national importance, and the project now being executed for their cheap transportation should be sufficiently provided for.

The Commission report that the results due to the still uncompleted works have been remarkable, and give the highest encouragement for expecting the ultimate success of the improvement.

The act of August 2, 1882, appropriated $4,123,000 for the work on that part of the river below Cairo. The estimates of the Commission already transmitted to Congress call for $3,000,000 for the continuation of the work below Cairo; and it appears from their report that all of the last appropriation available for active operations has been exhausted, and that there is urgently needed an immediate appropriation of $1,000,000 to continue the work without loss of time, in view of the approach of the flood season with its attendant dangers. I therefore recommend to Congress the early passage of a separate bill on this subject.

CHESTER A. ARTHUR.

Executive Mansion, *January 8, 1884.*

MESSAGE.

CESSION OF THE ILLINOIS AND MICHIGAN CANAL.

JANUARY 8, 1884.

235

MESSAGE.

To the Senate and House of Representatives:

I submit a communication from the governor of the State of Illinois, with a copy of an act of the general assembly of that State, tendering to the United States the cession of the Illinois and Michigan Canal, upon condition that it shall be enlarged and maintained as a national water-way for commercial purposes.

The proposed cession is an element of the subject which Congress had under consideration in directing, by the act of August 2, 1882, a survey for a canal from a point on the Illinois River at or near the town of Hennepin, by the most practicable route, to the Mississippi River at or above the city of Rock Island, the canal to be not less than seventy feet wide at the water line, and not less than seven feet in depth of water, and with capacity for vessels of at least two hundred and eighty tons burden; and also a survey of the Illinois and Michigan Canal, and an estimate of the cost of enlarging it to the dimensions of the proposed canal between Hennepin and the Mississippi River.

The surveys ordered in the above act have been completed, and the report upon them is included in the last Annual Report of the Secretary of War, and a copy is herewith submitted. It is estimated in the report that by the enlargement of the Illinois and Michigan Canal, and the construction of the proposed canal, by the shortest route, between Hennepin and the Mississippi River, a direct and convenient thoroughfare for vessels of two hundred and eighty tons burden may be opened from the Mississippi River to Lake Michigan, at a cost of $8,110,286.65, and that the annual charge for maintenance would be $138,600.

It appears from these papers that the estimated yield of corn, wheat, and oats for 1882, in the States of Illinois, Wisconsin, Iowa,

Minnesota, Kansas, and Nebraska, was more than a thousand million bushels. It is claimed that if the cheap water transportation route which is now continuous from the Atlantic Ocean to Chicago is extended to the Upper Mississippi by such a canal a great benefit in the reduction of freight charges would result to the people of the Upper Mississippi Valley, whose productions I have only partly noted, not only upon their own shipments, but upon the articles of commerce used by them which are now taken from the Eastern States by water only as far as Chicago.

As a matter of great interest, especially to the citizens of that part of the country, I commend the general subject to your consideration.

CHESTER A. ARTHUR.

EXECUTIVE MANSION, *January 8, 1884.*

MESSAGE

RELATIVE TO

THE RELIEF OF THE LADY FRANKLIN BAY EXPEDITION TO THE ARCTIC REGIONS.

JANUARY 17, 1884.

MESSAGE.

To the Senate and House of Representatives:

To the Senate and House of Representatives:

I transmit, for the consideration of Congress, a communication from the Secretary of War and the Secretary of the Navy on the subject of an expedition for the relief of Lieut. A. W. Greely and his party, composing what is known as the "Lady Franklin Bay Expedition," which was sent to the Arctic regions in 1881, under the provisions of the acts of Congress approved May 1, 1880, and March 3, 1881.

In the plans for the relief of this party, as arranged with Lieutenant Greely, it was contemplated that an effort would be made to communicate with him and furnish him any needed assistance in 1882, and again in 1883. Subsequently, legislation was enacted which required the expedition of 1883 to bring that party home. It was a part of the arrangement that if communication should not be made with him on or before the 1st of September, 1883, he should, with his party, abandon his station at Lady Franklin Bay not later than the above-mentioned date, and proceed southward, and would find a well-supplied relief-station at the entrance to Smith's Sound, a point where it would not be difficult to reach him during a part of each year.

The expeditions of 1882 and 1883 were sent; but neither one of them was able to communicate with Lieutenant Greely, and the last one failed to accomplish any part of its object beyond leaving a very small quantity of stores in the neighborhood of the entrance to Smith's Sound.

The situation of Lieutenant Greely and his party, under these circumstances, is one of great peril, and in presenting the preliminary views of the Board appointed by me to take into consideration an expedition for their relief, I urgently recommend prompt action by Congress to enable the recommendations of the Secretary of War and the Secretary of the Navy to be carried out without delay.

CHESTER A. ARTHUR.

EXECUTIVE MANSION,
 January 17, 1884.

EXECUTIVE MANSION, *December 17, 1883.*

The following-named officers of the Army and Navy will constitute a Board to consider an expedition to be sent for the relief of Lieutenant Greely and his party, composing what is known as the Lady Franklin Bay Expedition, and to recommend to the Secretaries of War and the Navy, jointly, the steps the Board may consider necessary to be taken for the equipment and transportation of the relief expedition, and to suggest such plan for its control and conduct, and for the organization of its *personnel*, as may seem to them best adapted to accomplish its purpose:

Brigadier-General William B. Hazen, Chief Signal Officer, United States Army.

Captain James A. Greer, United States Navy.

Lieutenant-Commander B. H. McCalla, United States Navy.

Captain George W. Davis, Fourteenth Infantry, United States Army.

The Board will meet in Washington, D. C., on the 20th instant.

CHESTER A. ARTHUR.

PROCLAMATION

CONCERNING

COMMERCIAL RELATIONS WITH SPAIN AND PORTO RICO.

FEBRUARY 14, 1884.

243

PROCLAMATION.

BY THE PRESIDENT OF THE UNITED STATES OF AMERICA.

A PROCLAMATION.

Whereas by a memorandum of an agreement executed at Madrid on the thirteenth day of February, A. D. one thousand eight hundred and eighty-four, by and between the duly authorized agents and representatives of the Government of the United States of America and of the Government of His Majesty the King of Spain, satisfactory evidence has been given to me that the Government of that country has abolished the discriminating customs duty heretofore imposed upon the products of, and articles proceeding from, the United States of America, imported into the islands of Cuba and Porto Rico, said abolition to take effect on and after the first day of March next:

Now, therefore, I, CHESTER A. ARTHUR, President of the United States of America, by virtue of the authority vested in me by section four thousand two hundred and twenty-eight of the Revised Statutes, do hereby declare and proclaim that, on and after the said first day of March next, so long as the products of, and articles proceeding from, the United States, imported into the islands of Cuba and Porto Rico, shall be exempt from discriminating customs duties, any such duties on the products of, and articles proceeding from Cuba and Porto Rico under the Spanish flag, shall be suspended and discontinued.

In witness whereof I have hereunto set my hand and caused the seal of the United States to be affixed.

245

Done at the city of Washington this fourteenth day of February, in the year of our Lord one thousand eight hundred and eighty-four, and of the Independence of the United States the one hundred and eighth.

[SEAL.]   CHESTER A. ARTHUR.

By the President:

FRED'K T. FRELINGHUYSEN,
Secretary of State.

MESSAGE

RELATIVE TO

THE GIFT BY THE BRITISH GOVERNMENT OF THE STEAMER ALERT FOR THE GREELY RELIEF EXPEDITION.

FEBRUARY 21, 1884.

MESSAGE.

I transmit herewith a report of the Secretary of State of the 21st instant whereby your honorable body, and through you the people of the United States may become apprised of the generous contribution made by Her Britannic Majesty's Government towards the efforts for the relief of Lieutenant Greely's Arctic exploring party by presenting to the United States the Arctic steamship Alert.

CHESTER A. ARTHUR.

Executive Mansion,
     February 21, 1884.

MESSAGE

REPORT OF THE CIVIL SERVICE COMMISSION.

FEBRUARY 29, 1884.

MESSAGE.

To the Senate and House of Representatives:

In compliance with the act of Congress approved January 16, 1883, entitled "An act to regulate and improve the civil service of the United States," the Civil Service Commission has made to the President its first annual report.

That report is herewith transmitted, together with communications from the heads of the several Executive Departments of the Government, respecting the practical working of the law under which the Commission has been acting.

Upon the good results which that law has already accomplished I congratulate Congress and the people, and I avow my conviction that it will henceforth prove to be of still more signal benefit to the public service.

I heartily commend the zeal and fidelity of the Commissioners and their suggestions for further legislation, and I advise the making of such an appropriation as shall be adequate for their needs.

CHESTER A. ARTHUR.

Executive Mansion,
February 29, 1884.

MESSAGE

CONCERNING

SWINE PRODUCTS OF THE UNITED STATES,

FEBRUARY 29, 1884.

255

MESSAGE.

To the House of Representatives:

I transmit herewith for the consideration of Congress a report of the Secretary of State, accompanying a report made by the Commission lately designated by me to examine and report upon the asserted unhealthfulness of the swine products of this country. The views and conclusions of the Commission deserve the most careful consideration of Congress, to the end that, if any path be legitimately open for removing the prohibition which closes important foreign markets to those products, it may be followed and appropriate legislation devised.

I earnestly recommend that Congress provide for reimbursing the expenses incurred by the Commissioners in this praiseworthy service, and I should be glad also if some remunerative recognition of their public-spirited action in accepting the onerous and responsible duties imposed on them were to suggest itself to Congress. At all events, in view of the conflicting theories touching the origin and propagation of trichiniasis and the means of isolating and extirpating it among domestic swine, and considering the important bearing which precise knowledge on these points would have on the commercial aspects of the matter, I recommend provision for special research in this direction.

CHESTER A. ARTHUR.

Executive Mansion,
Washington, February 29, 1884.

17*

MESSAGE.

INTERNATIONAL CONVENTION FOR THE PROTECTION OF INDUSTRIAL PROPERTY.

MARCH 11, 1884.

259

MESSAGE.

I submit herewith for the consideration of the Senate, with a view to obtaining its advice and consent thereto, a draft of a proclamation whereby the United States accede and adhere to an International Convention for the protection of industrial property, signed at Paris, March 20, 1883, and in explanation of the purport of that convention and the proposed mode of effecting the adhesion of the United States thereto, I subjoin a report of the Secretary of State.

CHESTER A. ARTHUR.

EXECUTIVE MANSION,
Washington, March 11, 1884.

MESSAGE.

RECONSTRUCTION OF THE NAVY.

MARCH 26, 1884.

MESSAGE.

In my annual message I impressed upon Congress the necessity of continued progress in the reconstruction of the Navy. The recommendations in this direction of the Secretary of the Navy and of the Naval Advisory Board were submitted by me, unaccompanied by specific expressions of approval. I now deem it my duty to advise that appropriations be made at the present session toward designing and commencing the construction of at least the three additional steel cruisers and the four gun-boats thus recommended, the cost of which, including their armament, will not exceed $4,283,000, of which sum one-half should be appropriated for the next fiscal year.

The Chicago, Boston, Atlanta, and Dolphin have been designed and are being built with care and skill, and there is every reason to believe that they will prove creditable and serviceable modern cruisers. Technical questions concerning the details of these or of additional vessels cannot wisely be settled except by experts; and the Naval Advisory Board organized by direction of Congress, under the act of August 5, 1882, and consisting of three line officers, a naval constructor, and a naval engineer, selected "with reference only to character, experience, knowledge, and skill," and a naval architect and a marine engineer from civil life, "of established reputation and standing as experts in naval or marine construction," is an appropriate authority to decide finally all such questions. I am unwilling to see the gradual reconstruction of our naval cruisers, now happily begun in conformity with modern requirements, delayed one full year for any unsubstantial reason.

Whatever conditions Congress may see fit to impose in order to secure judicious designs and honest and economical construction will be acceptable to me; but to relinquish or postpone the policy already deliberately declared will be, in my judgment, an act of national imprudence.

Appropriations should also be made without delay for finishing the four double-turreted monitors, the Puritan, Amphitrite, Terror, and Monadnock, and for procuring their armament and that of the Miantonomoh. Their hulls are built, and their machinery is under contract and approaching completion, except that of the Monadnock on the Pacific coast. This should also be built, and the armor and heavy guns of all should be procured at the earliest practicable moment.

The total amount appropriated up to this time for the four vessels is $3,546,941.41. A sum not exceeding $3,838,769.62, including $866,725 for four powerful rifled cannon and for the remainder of the ordnance outfit, will complete and equip them for service. Of the sum required only two millions need be appropriated for the next fiscal year. It is not expected that one of the monitors will be a match for the heaviest broadside iron-clads which certain other Governments have constructed at a cost of four or five millions each. But they will be armored vessels of an approved and useful type, presenting limited surfaces for the shot of an enemy, and possessed of such sea-going capacity and offensive power as fully to answer our immediate necessities. Their completion having been determined upon in the recent legislation of Congress, no time should be lost in accomplishing the necessary object.

The Gun Foundry Board, appointed by direction of Congress, consisting of three Army and three Navy officers, has submitted its report, duly transmitted on the 20th day of February, 1884, recommending that the Government should promote the production at private steel works of the required material for heavy cannon, and that two Government factories, one for the Army and one for the Navy, should be established for the fabrication of guns from such material. An early consideration of the report is recommended, together with such action as will enable the Government to construct its ordnance upon its own territory and so to provide the armaments demanded by considerations which concern the national safety and honor.

CHESTER A. ARTHUR.

EXECUTIVE MANSION,
    March 26, 1884.

MESSAGE.

MISSISSIPPI RIVER LEVEES.

APRIL 2, 1884.

267

MESSAGE.

TO THE SENATE AND HOUSE OF REPRESENTATIVES:

I transmit to Congress a communication from the Secretary of War, embodying the views of the President of the Mississippi River Commission upon a report from Major Stickney, of the Engineer Corps, in relation to the protection of existing levees from destruction by the floods in the lower part of the Mississippi River. It appears that there is an urgent need of an appropriation of $100,000 to be used for this purpose, and that an enormous destruction of property may be thereby averted.

I recommend an immediate appropriation of the sum required for the purpose, to be expended under the direction of the Mississippi River Commission.

CHESTER A. ARTHUR.

EXECUTIVE MANSION,
April 2, 1884.

269

EXECUTIVE ORDER

CONCERNING

THE WORLD'S INDUSTRIAL AND COTTON CENTENNIAL EXHIBITION.

APRIL 9, 1884.

271

EXECUTIVE ORDER.

BY THE PRESIDENT OF THE UNITED STATES.

EXECUTIVE ORDER.

Whereas it has been brought to the notice of the President of the United States that in the World's Industrial and Cotton Centennial Exhibition of Arts, Manufactures, and Products of the Soil and Mines, to be held in the city of New Orleans, commencing December 1, 1884, for the purpose of celebrating the one hundredth anniversary of the production, manufacture, and commerce of cotton, it is desirable that from the Executive Departments of the Government of the United States in which there may be articles suitable for the purpose intended, there should appear such articles and materials as will, when presented in a collection exhibition, illustrate the functions and administrative faculties of the Government in time of peace, and its resources as a war power, and thereby serve to demonstrate the nature of our institutions and their adaptation to the wants of the people: Now, for the purpose of securing a complete and harmonious arrangement of the articles and materials designed to be exhibited from the Executive Department of the Government, it is ordered that a Board, to be composed of one person to be named by the head of each of the Executive Departments which may have articles and materials to be exhibited, and also of one person to be named in behalf of the Smithsonian Institution, and one to be named in behalf of the Department of Agriculture, and one to be named in behalf of the Bureau of Education, be charged with the preparation, arrangement, and safe-keeping of such articles and materials as the heads of the several Departments and the Commissioner of Agriculture, the Director of the Smithsonian Institution, and the Commissioner of Education may respectively decide, shall be embraced in the collection; that one of the persons thus named,

MESSAGE

CONCERNING

SEA-COAST DEFENSES AND THEIR ARMAMENT.

APRIL 11, 1884.

MESSAGE

The condition of our sea-coast defenses and their armament has been brought to the attention of Congress in my annual messages, and I now submit a special estimate of the Chief of Ordnance, United States Army, transmitted by the Secretary of War, for a permanent annual appropriation of $1,500,000 to provide the necessary armament for our fortifications.

This estimate is founded upon the report of the Gun Foundry Board, recently transmitted, to which I have heretofore invited the early attention of Congress.

In presenting this estimate I do not think it necessary to enumerate the considerations which make it of the highest importance that there should be no unnecessary delay in entering upon the work, which must be commensurate with the public interests to be guarded and which will take much time.

CHESTER A. ARTHUR.

Executive Mansion,
April 11, 1884.

MESSAGE.

DEPARTMENT EXHIBIT FOR WORLD'S EXPOSITION AT NEW ORLEANS.

JUNE 9, 1884.

MESSAGE.

To the Senate and House of Representatives:

I transmit herewith, for the consideration of Congress, a letter and its accompanying estimate, submitted by the Board charged with preparing a Departmental exhibit for the World's Industrial and Cotton Centennial Exposition, to be held at New Orleans, beginning December 1, 1884. This Board was appointed by Executive order, of May 13, 1884, and is composed of representatives of the several Executive Departments, the Department of Agriculture, and the Smithsonian Institution. It is charged with the important and responsible duty of making arrangements for a complete and harmonious collection of the articles and materials deemed desirable to place on exhibition in illustration of the resources of the country, its methods of governmental administration, and its means of offense and defense.

The Board submits an estimate calling for an appropriation of $588,000 to accomplish the desired end. That amount is distributed among the Departments as shown in the table. The War, Navy, and Interior Departments call for the largest share, representing, as they do, the national defenses by land and sea, the progress of naval architecture and ordnance, the geological survey and mineral wealth of the Territories, the treatment of the Indians and the education of the masses, all of which admit of varied and instructive exhibits. The Smithsonian Institution, having under its general care the National Museum and the Fish Commission, is prepared to make a display second in interest to none of modern days. The remaining Departments can present instructive and interesting exhibits, which will attract popular attention and convey an idea of their extensively ramified duties, and of the many points where they beneficially affect the life of the people, as a nation and as individuals.

The exhibit of the Government at the Centennial Exhibition held at Philadelphia in 1876 was admitted to be one of the most attractive features of that great national undertaking, and a valuable addition to it. From men of intelligence and scientfic attainments at home and abroad it received the highest encomiums, showing the interest it awakened among those whose lives are given to the improvement of the social and material condition of the people.

The reproduction of such a display now on a more instructive plan is rendered possible by the advancement of science and invention during the eight years that have passed since the Philadelphia exhibit was collected.

The importance, purposes, and benefits of the New Orleans Exhibition are continental in their scope. Standing at the threshold of the almost unopened markets of Spanish and Portuguese America, New Orleans is a natural gateway to their trade, and the Exhibition offers to the people of Mexico and Central and South America an adequate knowledge of our farming implements, metal manufactures, cotton and woolen goods, and the like necessities of existence in respect to which those countries are either deficient or supplied to a limited extent. The breaking down of the barriers which still separate us from the Republics of America, whose productions so entirely complement our own, will aid greatly in removing the disparity of commercial intercourse, under which less than 10 per cent. of our exports goes to American countries.

I trust that Congress will realize the urgency of this recommendation and make its appropriation immediately available, so that the Board may lose no time in undertaking the extensive preparations necessary to spread a more intimate knowledge of our governmental institutions and national resources among the people of our country and of neighboring states, in a way to command the respect due it in the family of nations.

CHESTER A. ARTHUR.

EXECUTIVE MANSION,
   June 9, 1884.

MESSAGE.

SPECIAL LEGISLATION CONCERNING TAXATION IN THE DISTRICT OF COLUMBIA.

JUNE 21, 1884.

MESSAGE.

I have permitted House bill No. 4689, entitled "An act for the relief of Eliza W. Patterson," to become a law by withholding action upon it for ten days after it was presented to me.

The affairs and interests of the District of Columbia are committed to Congress as its Legislature. I do not question the constitutional right of Congress to pass a law relieving the family of an officer, in view of the services he had rendered his country, from the burdens of taxation, but I submit to Congress that this just gift of the nation to the family of such faithful officer should come from the national Treasury rather than from that of this District, and I therefore recommend that an appropriation be made to reimburse the District for the amount of taxes which would have been due to it had this act not become a law.

CHESTER A. ARTHUR.

Executive Mansion,
June 21, 1884.

285

MESSAGE.

THE FITZ-JOHN PORTER BILL.

JULY 2, 1884.

MESSAGE.

To the House of Representatives:

After careful consideration of the bill entitled "An act for the relief of Fitz-John Porter," I herewith return it with my objections to that house of Congress in which it originated. Its enacting clause is in terms following:

"That the President be, and he is hereby, authorized to nominate and, by and with the advice and consent of the Senate, to appoint Fitz-John Porter, late a major-general of the United States volunteers, and a brevet brigadier-general and colonel of the Army, to the position of colonel in the Army of the United States, of the same grade and rank held by him at the time of his dismissal from the Army by sentence of court-martial, promulgated January 27, 1863," &c.

It is apparent that should this bill become a law it will create a new office, which can be filled by the appointment of the particular individual whom it specifies, and can not be filled otherwise; or it may be said with perhaps greater precision of statement that it will create a new office upon condition that the particular person designated shall be chosen to fill it. Such an act, as it seems to me, is either unnecessary and ineffective, or it involves an encroachment by the legislative branch of the Government upon the authority of the Executive. As the Congress has no power under the Constitution to nominate or appoint an officer, and cannot lawfully impose upon the President the duty of nominating or appointing to office any particular individual of its own selection, this bill, if it can fairly be construed as requiring the President to make the nomination and, by and with the advice and consent of the Senate, the appointment which it authorizes, is in manifest violation of the Constitution. If such be not its just interpretation, it must be regarded as a mere enactment of advice and counsel, which lacks in the very nature of things the force of positive law, and can serve no useful purpose upon the statute-books.

There are other causes that deter me from giving this bill the sanction of my approval. The judgment of the court-martial by which more than twenty years since General Fitz-John Porter was tried and convicted was pronounced by a tribunal composed of nine general officers of distinguished character and ability. Its investigation of the charges of which it found the accused guilty was thorough and conscientious, and its findings and sentence were in due course of law approved by Abraham Lincoln, then President of the United States. Its legal competency, its jurisdiction of the accused and of the subject of the accusation, and the substantial regularity of all its proceedings, are matters which have never been brought in question. Its judgment, therefore, is final and conclusive in its character.

The Supreme Court of the United States has recently declared that a court-martial such as this was is the organism provided by law and clothed with the duty of administering justice in this class of cases. Its judgments, when approved, rest on the same basis and are surrounded by the same considerations which give conclusiveness to the judgments of other legal tribunals, including as well the lowest as the highest. It follows, accordingly, that when a lawfully consti-tuted court-martial has duly declared its findings and its sentence, and the same have been duly approved, neither the President nor the Congress has any power to set them aside. The existence of such power is not openly asserted, nor perhaps is it necessarily im-plied, in the provisions of the bill which is before me, but when its enacting clauses are read in the light of the recitations of its pream-ble it will be seen that it seeks in effect the practical annulment of the findings and the sentence of a competent court-martial.

A conclusion at variance with these findings has been reached after investigation by a board consisting of three officers of the Army. This board was not created in pursuance of any statutory authority, and was powerless to compel the attendance of witnesses or to pro-nounce a judgment which could have been lawfully enforced. The officers who constituted it in their report to the Secretary of War, dated March 19, 1879, state that in their opinion "justice requires * * * such action as may be necessary to annul and set aside the findings and sentence of the court-martial in the case of Maj. Gen. Fitz-John Porter, and to restore him to the positions of which that sentence deprived him, such restoration to take effect from the date of his dismissal from the service.''

The provisions of the bill now under consideration are avowedly based on the assumption that the findings of the court-martial have been discovered to be erroneous. But it will be borne in mind that the investigation which is claimed to have resulted in this discovery was made many years after the events to which that evidence related, and under circumstances that made it impossible to reproduce the evidence on which they were based.

It seems to me that the proposed legislation would establish a dangerous precedent, calculated to imperil in no small measure the binding force and effect of the judgments of the various tribunals established under our Constitution and laws.

I have already, in the exercise of the pardoning power with which the President is vested by the Constitution remitted the continuing penalty which had made it impossible for Fitz-John Porter to hold any office of trust or profit under the Government of the United States. But I am unwilling to give my sanction to any legislation which shall practically annul and set at naught the solemn and deliberate conclusions of the tribunal by which he was convicted and of the President by whom its findings were examined and approved.

CHESTER A. ARTHUR.

EXECUTIVE MANSION,
July 2, 1884.

PROCLAMATION

APPOINTING

THURSDAY, NOVEMBER 27, 1884, AS A DAY OF NATIONAL THANKSGIVING.

NOVEMBER 7, 1884.

293

PROCLAMATION.

BY THE PRESIDENT OF THE UNITED STATES OF AMERICA.

A PROCLAMATION.

The season is nigh when it is the yearly wont of this people to observe a day appointed for that purpose by the President, as an especial occasion for thanksgiving unto God:

Now, therefore, in recognition of this hallowed custom, I, CHESTER A. ARTHUR, President of the United States, do hereby designate as such day of general thanksgiving, Thursday the 27th day of this present November.

And I do recommend that throughout the land, the people ceasing from their accustomed occupations, do then keep holiday at their several homes and their several places of worship, and with heart and voice pay reverent acknowledgment to the Giver of all good for the countless blessings wherewith He hath visited this nation.

In witness whereof I have hereunto set my hand and caused the seal of the United States to be affixed.

Done at the city of Washington this seventh day of November, in the year of our Lord one thousand eight hundred and eighty-four, and of the Independence of the United States the one hundred and ninth.

[SEAL.]   CHESTER A. ARTHUR.

By the President:

FRED'K T. FRELINGHUYSEN,
Secretary of State.

MESSAGE

TO THE

SENATE AND HOUSE OF REPRESENTATIVES,

DECEMBER 1, 1884.

MESSAGE.

Since the close of your last session the American people, in the exercise of their highest right of suffrage, have chosen their Chief Magistrate for the four years ensuing.

When it is remembered that at no period in the country's history has the long political contest which customarily precedes the day of the national election been waged with greater fervor and intensity, it is a subject of general congratulation that after the controversy at the polls was over, and while the slight preponderance by which the issue had been determined was as yet unascertained, the public peace suffered no disturbance, but the people everywhere patiently and quietly awaited the result.

Nothing could more strikingly illustrate the temper of the American citizen, his love of order, and his loyalty to law—nothing could more signally demonstrate the strength and wisdom of our political institutions.

Eight years have passed since a controversy concerning the result of a national election sharply called the attention of the Congress to the necessity of providing more precise and definite regulations for counting the electoral vote.

It is of the gravest importance that this question be solved before conflicting claims to the Presidency shall again distract the country, and I am persuaded that, by the people at large, any of the measures of relief thus far proposed would be preferred to continued inaction.

Our relations with all foreign powers continue to be amicable.

With Belgium a convention has been signed whereby the scope of present treaties has been so enlarged as to secure to citizens of either country within the jurisdiction of the othe: equal rights and privileges in the acquisition and alienation of property. A trade-marks treaty has also been concluded.

The war between Chili and Peru is at an end. For the arbitration of the claims of American citizens who during its continuance suffered through the acts of the Chilian authorities a convention will soon be negotiated.

The state of hostilities between France and China continues to be an embarrassing feature of our Eastern relations. The Chinese Government has promptly adjusted and paid the claims of American citizens whose property was destroyed in the recent riots at Canton. I renew the recommendation of my last annual message,· that the Canton indemnity fund be returned to China.

The true interpretation of the recent treaty with that country, permitting the restriction of Chinese immigration, is likely to be again the subject of your deliberations. It may be seriously questioned whether the statute passed at the last session does not violate the treaty rights of certain Chinese who left this country with return certificates valid under the old law and who now seem to be debarred from relanding for lack of the certificates required by the new.

The recent purchase by citizens of the United States of a large trading fleet heretofore under the Chinese flag has considerably enhanced our commercial importance in the East. In view of the large number of vessels built or purchased by American citizens in other countries and exclusively employed in legitimate traffic between foreign ports under the recognized protection of our flag, it might be well to provide a uniform rule for their registration and documentation, so that the *bona fide* property rights of our citizens therein shall be duly evidenced and properly guarded.

Pursuant to the advice of the Senate at the last session, I recognized the flag of the International Association of the Congo as that of a friendly Government, avoiding in so doing any prejudgment of conflicting territorial claims in that region. Subsequently, in execution of the expressed wish of the Congress, I appointed a commercial agent for the Congo Basin.

The importance of the rich prospective trade of the Congo Valley has led to the general conviction that it should be open to all nations upon equal terms. At an international conference for the consideration of this subject called by the Emperor of Germany, and now in session at Berlin, delegates are in attendance on behalf of the United States. Of the results of the conference you will be duly advised.

The Government of Corea has generously aided the efforts of the United States minister to secure suitable premises for the use of the legation. As the conditions of diplomatic intercourse with Eastern nations demand that the legation premises be owned by the represented power, I advise that an appropriation be made for the acquisition of this property by the Government. The United States already possess valuable premises at Tangier as a gift from the Sultan of Morocco. As is stated hereafter, they have lately received a similar gift from the Siamese Government. The Government of Japan stands ready to present to us extensive grounds at Tokio whereon to erect a suitable building for the legation, court-house, and jail; and similar privileges can probably be secured in China and Persia. The owning of such premises would not only effect a large saving of the present rentals but would permit of the due assertion of extraterritorial rights in those countries, and would the better serve to maintain the dignity of the United States.

The failure of Congress to make appropriation for our representation at the autonomous court of the Khedive has proved a serious embarrassment in our intercourse with Egypt ; and in view of the necessary intimacy of diplomatic relationship due to the participation of this Government, as one of the treaty powers, in all matters of administration there affecting the rights of foreigners, I advise the restoration of the agency and consulate-general at Cairo on its former basis. I do not conceive it to be the wish of Congress that the United States should withdraw altogether from the honorable position they have hitherto held with respect to the Khedive, or that citizens of this Republic residing or sojourning in Egypt should hereafter be without the aid and protection of a competent representative.

With France, the traditional cordial relationship continues. The colossal statue of Liberty enlightening the World, the generous gift

spirit which has prompted this gift, and in aid of the timely completion of the pedestal upon which it is to be placed.

Our relations with Germany, a country which contributes to our own some of the best elements of citizenship, continue to be cordial. The United States have extradition treaties with several of the German states, but by reason of the confederation of those states under the Imperial rule, the application of such treaties is not as uniform and comprehensive as the interests of the two countries require. I propose, therefore, to open negotiations for a single convention of extradition to embrace all the territory of the Empire.

It affords me pleasure to say that our intercourse with Great Brit-

The revolution in Hayti against the established Government has terminated. While it was in progress it became necessary to enforce our neutrality laws by instituting proceedings against individuals and vessels charged with their infringement. These prosecutions were in all cases successful.

Much anxiety has lately been displayed by various European Governments, and especially by the Government of Italy, for the abolition of our import duties upon works of art. It is well to consider whether the present discrimination in favor of the productions of American artists abroad is not likely to result, as they themselves seem very generally to believe it may, in the practical exclusion of our painters and sculptors from the rich fields for observation, study, and labor which they have hitherto enjoyed.

There is prospect that the long-pending revision of the foreign treaties of Japan may be concluded at a new conference to be held at Tokio. While this Government fully recognizes the equal and independent station of Japan in the community of nations, it would not oppose the general adoption of such terms of compromise as Japan may be disposed to offer in furtherance of a uniform policy of intercourse with Western nations.

During the past year the increasing good-will between our own Government and that of Mexico has been variously manifested. The treaty of commercial reciprocity concluded January 20, 1883, has been ratified, and awaits the necessary tariff legislation of Congress to become effective. This legislation will, I doubt not, be among the first measures to claim your attention.

A full treaty of commerce, navigation, and consular rights is much to be desired, and such a treaty I have reason to believe that the Mexican Government stands ready to conclude.

Some embarrassment has been occasioned by the failure of Congress at its last session to provide means for the due execution of the treaty of July 29, 1882, for the resurvey of the Mexican boundary and the relocation of boundary monuments.

With the Republic of Nicaragua a treaty has been concluded which authorizes the construction by the United States of a canal, railway, and telegraph line across the Nicaraguan territory.

By the terms of this treaty sixty miles of the river San Juan, as well as Lake Nicaragua, an inland sea forty miles in width, are to constitute a part of the projected enterprise.

This leaves for actual canal construction seventeen miles on the Pacific side and thirty-six miles on the Atlantic. To the United States, whose rich territory on the Pacific is for the ordinary purposes of commerce practically cut off from communication by water with the Atlantic ports, the political and commercial advantages of such a project can scarcely be overestimated.

It is believed that when the treaty is laid before you the justice and liberality of its provisions will command universal approval at home and abroad.

The death of our representative at Russia while at his post at St. Petersburg afforded to the Imperial Government a renewed opportunity to testify its sympathy in a manner befitting the intimate friendliness which has ever marked the intercourse of the two countries.

The course of this Government in raising its representation at Bangkok to the diplomatic rank has evoked from Siam evidences of warm friendship and augurs well for our enlarged intercourse. The Siamese Government has presented to the United States a commodious mansion and grounds for the occupancy of the legation, and I suggest that by joint resolution Congress attest its appreciation of this generous gift.

This Government has more than once been called upon of late to take action in fulfillment of its international obligations toward Spain. Agitation in the island of Cuba hostile to the Spanish Crown having been fomented by persons abusing the sacred rights of hospitality which our territory affords, the officers of this Government have been instructed to exercise vigilance to prevent infractions of our neutrality laws at Key West and at other points near the Cuban coast. I am happy to say that in the only instance where these precautionary measures were successfully eluded, the offenders when found in our territory were subsequently tried and convicted.

The growing need of close relationship of intercourse and traffic between the Spanish Antilles and their natural market in the United States led to the adoption, in January last, of a commercial agreement looking to that end. This agreement has since been superseded by a more carefully framed and comprehensive convention, which I shall submit to the Senate for approval. It has been the aim of this negotiation to open such a favored reciprocal exchange of productions carried under the flag of either country, as to make the intercourse between Cuba and Porto Rico and ourselves scarcely less intimate than the commercial movement between our domestic ports, and to insure a removal of the burdens on shipping in the Spanish Indies, of which in the past our ship-owners and ship-masters have so often had cause to complain.

The negotiation of this convention has for a time postponed the prosecution of certain claims of our citizens which were declared to be without the jurisdiction of the late Spanish-American Claims Commission, and which are therefore remitted to diplomatic channels for adjustment. The speedy settlement of these claims will now be urged by this Government.

Negotiations for a treaty of commercial reciprocity with the Dominican Republic have been successfully concluded, and the result will shortly be laid before the Senate.

Certain questions between the United States and the Ottoman Empire still remain unsolved. Complaints on behalf of our citizens are not satisfactorily adjusted. The Porte has sought to withhold from our commerce the right of favored treatment to which we are entitled by existing conventional stipulations, and the revision of the tariffs is unaccomplished.

The final disposition of pending questions with Venezuela has not as yet been reached, but I have good reason to expect an early settlement, which will provide the means of re-examining the Caracas awards in conformity with the expressed desire of Congress, and which will recognize the justice of certain claims preferred against Venezuela.

The Central and South American Commission appointed by authority of the act of July 7, 1884, will soon proceed to Mexico. It has been furnished with instructions which will be laid before you. They contain a statement of the general policy of the Government for enlarging its commercial intercourse with American States. The commissioners have been actively preparing for their responsible task by holding conferences in the principal cities with merchants and others interested in Central and South American trade.

The International Meridian Conference, lately convened in Washington upon the invitation of the Government of the United States, was composed of representatives from twenty-five nations. The conference concluded its labors on the 1st of November, having with substantial unanimity agreed upon the meridian of Greenwich as the starting point whence longitude is to be computed through one hundred and eighty degrees eastward and westward, and upon the adoption, for all purposes for which it may be found convenient, of a universal day which shall begin at midnight on the initial meridian and whose hours shall be counted from zero up to twenty-four.

20*

The formal report of the transactions of this conference will be hereafter transmitted to the Congress.

This Government is in frequent receipt of invitations from foreign states to participate in international exhibitions, often of great interest and importance. Occupying as we do an advanced position in the world's production, and aiming to secure a profitable share for our industries in the general competitive markets, it is a matter of serious concern that the want of means for participation in these exhibitions should so often exclude our producers from advantages enjoyed by those of other countries. During the past year the attention of Congress was drawn to the formal invitations in this regard tendered by the Governments of England, Holland, Belgium, Germany, and Austria. The Executive has in some instances appointed honorary commissioners. This is, however, a most unsatisfactory expedient, for without some provision to meet the necessary working expenses of a commission it can effect little or nothing in behalf of exhibitors. An international inventions exhibition is to be held in London next May. This will cover a field of special importance, in which our country holds a foremost rank, but the Executive is at present powerless to organize a proper representation of our vast national interests in this direction.

I have in several previous messages referred to this subject. It seems to me that a statute, giving to the Executive general discretionary authority to accept such invitations, and to appoint honorary commissioners, without salary, and placing at the disposal of the Secretary of State a small fund for defraying their reasonable expenses, would be of great public utility.

This Government has received official notice that the Revised International Regulations for preventing collisions at sea have been adopted by all the leading maritime powers except the United States, and came into force on the 1st of September last. For the due protection of our shipping interests, the provisions of our statutes should at once be brought into conformity with these Regulations.

The question of securing to authors, composers, and artists copyright privileges in this country in return for reciprocal rights abroad is one that may justly challenge your attention. It is true that conventions will be necessary for fully accomplishing this result, but until Congress shall by statute fix the extent to which foreign holders of copyright shall be here privileged, it has been deemed inadvisable to negotiate such conventions. For this reason the United States were not represented at the recent conference at Berne.

I recommend that the scope of the neutrality laws of the United States be so enlarged as to cover all patent acts of hostility committed in our territory and aimed against the peace of a friendly nation. Existing statutes prohibit the fitting out of armed expeditions and restrict the shipment of explosives, though the enactments in the latter respect were not framed with regard to international obligations, but simply for the protection of passenger travel. All these statutes were intended to meet special emergencies that had already arisen. Other emergencies have arisen since, and modern ingenuity supplies means for the organization of hostilities without open resort to armed vessels or to filibustering parties.

I see no reason why overt preparations in this country for the commission of criminal acts, such as are here under consideration, should not be alike punishable, whether such acts are intended to be committed in our own country or in a foreign country with which we are at peace.

The prompt and thorough treatment of this question is one which intimately concerns the national honor.

Our existing naturalization laws also need revision. Those sections relating to persons residing within the limits of the United States in 1795 and 1798 have now only a historical interest. Section 2172, recognizing the citizenship of the children of naturalized parents, is ambiguous in its terms and partly obsolete. There are special provisions of law favoring the naturalization of those who serve in the Army or in merchant vessels, while no similar privileges are granted those who serve in the Navy or the Marine Corps.

"An uniform rule of naturalization," such as the Constitution contemplates, should, among other things, clearly define the status of persons born within the United States subject to a foreign power (section 1992) and of minor children of fathers who have declared their intention to become citizens but have failed to perfect their naturalization.   It might be wise to provide for a central bureau of registry, wherein should be filed authenticated transcripts of every record of naturalization in the several Federal and State courts, and to make provision also for the vacation or cancellation of such record in cases where fraud had been practiced upon the court by the applicant himself or where he had renounced or forfeited his acquired citizenship.   A just and uniform law in this respect would strengthen the hands of the Government in protecting its citizens abroad, and would pave the way for the conclusion of treaties of naturalization with foreign countries.

The legislation of the last session effected in the diplomatic and consular service certain changes and reductions which have been productive of embarrassment.   The population and commercial activity of our country are steadily on the increase, and are giving rise to new, varying, and often delicate relationships with other countries.   Our foreign establishment now embraces nearly double the area of operations that it occupied twenty years ago.   The confinement of such a service within the limits of expenditure then established is not, it seems to me, in accordance with true economy. A community of sixty millions of people should be adequately represented in its intercourse with foreign nations.

A project for the reorganization of the consular service and for recasting the scheme of extraterritorial jurisdiction is now before you.   If the limits of a short session will not allow of its full consideration, I trust that you will not fail to make suitable provision for the present needs of the service.

It has been customary to define in the appropriation acts the rank of each diplomatic office to which a salary is attached.   I suggest that this course be abandoned and that it be left to the President, with the advice and consent of the Senate, to fix from time to time the diplomatic grade of the representatives of this Government abroad as may seem advisable, provision being definitely made, however, as now for the amount of salary attached to the respective stations

The condition of our finances and the operations of the various branches of the public service which are connected with the Treasury Department are very fully discussed in the report of the Secretary.

It appears that the ordinary revenues for the fiscal year ended June 30, 1884, were—

From customs	$195,067,489 76
From internal revenue	121,586,072 51
From all other sources	31,866,307 65
Total ordinary revenues.........................	348,519,869 92

The public expenditures during the same period were—

For civil expenses............	$22,312,907 71
For foreign intercourse............ ....•.........	1,260,766 37
For Indians..................	6,475,999 29
For pensions...	55,429,228 06
For the military establishment, including river and harbor improvements and arsenals............	39,429,603 36
For the naval establishment, including vessels, machinery, and improvements at navy-yards ...	17,292,601 44
For miscellaneous expenditures, including public buildings, light-houses, and collecting the revenue	43,939,710 00
For expenditures on account of the District of Columbia	3,407,049 62
For interest on the public debt	54,578,378 48
For the sinking fund	46,790,229 50
Total ordinary expenditures...................	290,916,473 83
Leaving a surplus of..............................	57,603,396 09

As compared with the preceding fiscal year there was a net decrease of over $21,000,000 in the amount of expenditures. The aggregate receipts were less than those of the year previous by about $54,000,000. The falling off in revenue from customs made up nearly $20,000,000 of this deficiency, and about $23,000,000 of the remainder was due to the diminished receipts from internal taxation.

The Secretary estimates the total receipts for the fiscal year which will end June 30, 1885, at $330,000,000, and the total expenditures at $290,620,201.16, in which sum are included the interest on the debt and the amount payable to the sinking fund.   This would

during the year ending June 30, 1884, was as follows:

Domestic merchandise	$724,964,852
Foreign merchandise	15,548,757
	740,513,609
	67,133,383
Total exports of merchandise and specie	807,646,992

The cotton and cotton manufactures included in this statement were valued at $208,900,415; the breadstuffs at $162,544,715; the provisions at $114,416,547, and the mineral oils at $47,103,248.

During the same period the imports were as follows:

Merchandise	$667,697,693
Gold and silver	37,426,262
Total	705,123,955

More than 63 per cent. of the entire value of imported merchandise consisted of the following articles:

Sugar and molasses	$103,884,274
Wool and woolen manufactures	53,542,292
Silk and its manufactures	49,949,128
Coffee	49,686,705
Iron and steel and manufactures thereof	41,464,599
Chemicals	38,464,965
Flax, hemp, jute, and like substances, and manufactures thereof	33,463,398
Cotton and manufactures of cotton	30,454,476
Hides and skins other than fur-skins	22,350,906

I concur with the Secretary of the Treasury in recommending the immediate suspension of the coinage of silver dollars and of the issuance of silver certificates.   This is a matter to which, in former communications, I have more than once invoked the attention of the National Legislature.

It appears that annually for the past six years there have been coined, in compliance with the requirements of the act of February 28, 1878, more than twenty-seven million silver dollars.   The number now outstanding is reported by the Secretary to be nearly one hundred and eighty-five million, whereof but little more than forty million, or less than 22 per cent., are in actual circulation.   The mere existence of this fact seems to me to furnish of itself a cogent argument for the repeal of the statute which has made such fact possible.

But there are other and graver considerations that tend in the same direction.

The Secretary avows his conviction that unless this coinage and the issuance of silver certificates be suspended, silver is likely at no distant day to become our sole metallic standard.   The commercial disturbance and the impairment of national credit that would be thus occasioned can scarcely be overestimated.

I hope that the Secretary's suggestions respecting the withdrawal from circulation of the one-dollar and two-dollar notes will receive your approval.   It is likely that a considerable portion of the silver now encumbering the vaults of the Treasury might thus find its way into the currency.

While trade-dollars have ceased, for the present at least, to be an element of active disturbance in our currency system, some provision should be made for their surrender to the Government.   In view of the circumstances under which they were coined and of the fact that they have never had a legal-tender quality, there should be offered for them only a slight advance over their bullion value.

The Secretary, in the course of his report, considers the propriety of beautifying the designs of our subsidiary silver coins and of so increasing their weight that they may bear their due ratio of value to the standard dollar.   His conclusions in this regard are cordially approved.

In my annual message of 1882, I recommended the abolition of all excise taxes except those relating to distilled spirits.   This rec-

ished, the revenues that will still remain to the Government will, in my opinion, not only suffice to meet its reasonable expenditures, but will afford a surplus large enough to permit such tariff reduction as may seem to be advisable, when the results of recent revenue laws and commercial treaties shall have shown in what quarters those reductions can be most judiciously effected.

One of the gravest of the problems which appeal to the wisdom of Congress for solution is the ascertainment of the most effective means for increasing our foreign trade and thus relieving the de-

Secretary of the Treasury advises that the duty of investigating this subject be intrusted in the first instance to a competent commission. While fully recognizing the considerations that may be urged against this course, I am nevertheless of the opinion that, upon the whole, no other would be likely to effect speedier or better results.

That portion of the Secretary's report which concerns the condition of our shipping interests cannot fail to command your attention. He emphatically recommends that as an incentive to the investment of American capital in American steamships, the Government shall by liberal payments for mail transportation, or otherwise, lend its active assistance to individual enterprise, and declares his belief that unless that course be pursued our foreign carrying trade must remain, as it is to-day, almost exclusively in the hands of foreigners.

One phase of this subject is now especially prominent, in view of the repeal by the act of June 26, 1884, of all statutory provisions arbitrarily compelling American vessels to carry the mails to and from the United States. As it is necessary to make provision to compensate the owners of such vessels for performing that service after April, 1885, it is hoped that the whole subject will receive early consideration that will lead to the enactment of such measures for the revival of our merchant marine as the wisdom of Congress may devise.

The three per cent. bonds of the Government to the amount of more than $100,000,000 have, since my last annual message, been redeemed by the Treasury. The bonds of that issue still outstanding amount to little over $200,000,000, about one-fourth of which will be retired through the operations of the sinking fund during the coming year. As these bonds still constitute the chief basis for the circulation of the national banks, the question how to avert the contraction of the currency, caused by their retirement, is one of constantly increasing importance.

It seems to be generally conceded that the law governing this matter exacts from the banks excessive security, and that, upon their present bond deposits, a larger circulation than is now allowed may be granted with safety. I hope that the bill which passed the Senate at the last session, permitting the issue of notes equal to the face value of the deposited bonds, will commend itself to the approval of the House of Representatives.

In the expenses of the War Department the Secretary reports a decrease of more than $9,000,000. Of this reduction $5,600,000 was effected in the expenditures for rivers and harbors, and $2,700,000 in expenditures for the Quartermaster's Department.

Outside of that Department the annual expenses of all the Army bureaus proper (except possibly the Ordnance Bureau) are substantially fixed charges, which can not be materially diminished without a change in the numerical strength of the Army. The expenditures in the Quartermaster's Department can readily be subjected to administrative discretion, and it is reported by the Secretary of War that as a result of exercising such discretion, in reducing the number of draught and pack animals in the Army, the annual cost of supplying and caring for such animals is now $1,108,085.90 less than it was in 1881.

The reports of military commanders show that the last year has been notable for its entire freedom from Indian outbreaks.

In defiance of the President's proclamation of July 1, 1884, certain intruders sought to make settlements in the Indian Territory. They were promptly removed by a detachment of troops.

During the past session of Congress a bill to provide a suitable fire-proof building for the Army Medical Museum and the library of the Surgeon-General's Office received the approval of the Senate. A similar bill, reported favorably to the House of Representatives by one of its committees, is still pending before that body. It is hoped that during the coming session the measure may become a law, and that thereafter immediate steps may be taken to secure a place of safe deposit for these valuable collections, now in a state of insecurity.

The funds with which the works for the improvement of rivers and harbors were prosecuted during the past year were derived from the appropriations of the act of August 2, 1882, together with such few balances as were on hand from previous appropriations. The balance in the Treasury subject to requisition July 1, 1883, was $10,021,649.55. The amount appropriated during the fiscal year 1884 was $1,319,634.62, and the amount drawn from the Treasury during the fiscal year was $8,228,703.54, leaving a balance of $3,112,580.63 in the Treasury subject to requisition July 1, 1884.

The Secretary of War submits the report of the Chief of Engineers as to the practicability of protecting our important cities on the sea-board by fortifications and other defenses able to repel modern methods of attack. The time has now come when such defenses can be prepared with confidence that they will not prove abortive; and, when the possible result of delay in making such preparation is seriously considered, delay seems inexcusable. For the most important cities—those whose destruction or capture would be a national humiliation—adequate defenses, inclusive of guns, may be made by the gradual expenditure of $60,000,000, a sum much less than a victorious enemy could levy as a contribution. An appropriation of about one-tenth of that amount is asked to begin the work, and I concur with the Secretary of War in urging that it be granted.

The War Department is proceeding with the conversion of 10-inch smooth-bore guns into 8-inch rifles, by lining the former with tubes of forged steel or of coiled wrought-iron. Fifty guns will be thus converted within the year. This, however, does not obviate the necessity of providing means for the construction of guns of the highest power, both for the purposes of coast defense and for the armament of war vessels.

The report of the Gun Foundery Board, appointed April 2, 1883, in pursuance of the act of March 3, 1883, was transmitted to Congress in a special message of February 18, 1884. In my message of March

26, 1884, I called attention to the recommendation of the Board that the Government should encourage the production at private steel works of the required material for heavy cannon, and that two Government factories, one for the Army and one for the Navy, should be established for the fabrication of guns from such material. No action having been taken, the Board was subsequently reconvened to determine more fully the plans and estimates necessary for carrying out its recommendation. It has received information which indicates that there are responsible steel manufacturers in this country who, although not provided at present with the necessary plant, are willing to construct the same and to make bids for contracts with the Government for the supply of the requisite material for the heaviest guns adapted to modern warfare, if a guaranteed order of sufficient magnitude, accompanied by a positive appropriation extending over a series of years, shall be made by Congress. All doubts as to the feasibility of the plan being thus removed, I renew my recommendation that such action be taken by Congress as will enable the Government to construct its own ordnance upon its own territory, and so to provide the armaments demanded by considerations of national safety and honor.

The report of the Secretary of the Navy exhibits the progress which has been made on the new steel cruisers authorized by the acts of August 5, 1882, and March 3, 1883. Of the four vessels under contract, one, the Chicago, of 4,500 tons, is more than half finished; the Atlanta, of 3,000 tons, has been successfully launched, and her machinery is now fitting; the Boston, also of 3,000 tons, is ready for launching, and the Dolphin, a dispatch steamer of 1,500 tons, is ready for delivery.

Certain adverse criticisms upon the designs of these cruisers are discussed by the Secretary, who insists that the correctness of the conclusions reached by the Advisory Board and by the Department has been demonstrated by recent developments in ship-building abroad.

The machinery of the double-turreted monitors Puritan, Terror, and Amphitrite, contracted for under the act of March 3, 1883, is in process of construction. No work has been done during the past year on their armor for lack of the necessary appropriations. A fourth monitor, the Monadnock, still remains unfinished at the navy-yard in California. It is recommended that early steps be taken to complete these vessels and to provide also an armament for the mon-

The recommendations of the Naval Advisory Board, approved by the Department, comprise the construction of one steel cruiser of 4,500 tons, one cruiser of 3,000 tons, two heavily-armed gunboats, one light cruising gunboat, one dispatch-vessel armed with Hotch-

eral designs, all of which are calculated to meet the existing wants of the service, are now well advanced, and the construction of the

their grave in the Lena Delta in March, 1883, and were retained at Yakutsk until the following winter, the season being too far advanced to admit of their immediate transportation. They arrived at New York February 20, 1884, where they were received with suitable honors.

In pursuance of the joint resolution of Congress approved February 13, 1884, a naval expedition was fitted out for the relief of Lieut. A. W. Greely, United States Army, and of the party who had been engaged under his command in scientific observations at Lady Franklin Bay. The fleet consisted of the steam sealer Thetis, purchased in England, the Bear, purchased at St. John's, Newfoundland, and the Alert, which was generously provided by the British Government. Preparations for the expedition were promptly made by the Secretary of the Navy, with the active co-operation of the Secretary of War. Commander George W. Coffin was placed in command of the Alert, and Lieut. William H. Emory in command of the Bear. The Thetis was intrusted to Commander Winfield S.

Schley, to whom also was assigned the superintendence of the entire expedition.

Immediately upon its arrival at Upernavik, the fleet began the dangerous navigation of Melville Bay, and in spite of every obstacle reached Littleton Island on June 22, a fortnight earlier than any vessel had before attained that point. On the same day it crossed over to Cape Sabine, where Lieutenant Greely and the other survivors of his party were discovered. After taking on board the living and the bodies of the dead, the relief ships sailed for St. John's, where they arrived on July 17. They were appropriately received at Portsmouth, N. H., on August 1, and at New York on August 8. One of the bodies was landed at the former place. The others were put on shore at Governor's Island, and, with the exception of one which was interred in the National Cemetery, were forwarded thence to the destinations indicated by friends. The organization and conduct of this Relief Expedition reflects great credit upon all who contributed to its success.

In this, the last of the stated messages that I shall have the honor to transmit to the Congress of the United States, I cannot too strongly urge upon its attention the duty of restoring our Navy as rapidly as possible to the high state of efficiency which formerly characterized it. As the long peace that has lulled us into a sense of fancied security may at any time be disturbed, it is plain that the policy of strengthening this arm of the service is dictated by considerations of wise economy, of just regard for our future tranquillity, and of true appreciation of the dignity and honor of the Republic.

The report of the Postmaster-General acquaints you with the present condition and needs of the postal service.

It discloses the gratifying fact that the loss of revenue from the reduction in the rate of letter-postage recommended in my message of December 4, 1882, and effected by the act of March 3, 1883, has been much less than was generally anticipated. My recommendation of this reduction was based upon the belief that the actual falling off in receipts from letter-postages for the year immediately succeeding the change of rate would be $3,000,000. It has proved to be only $2,275,000.

This is a trustworthy indication that the revenue will soon be restored to its former volume by the natural increase of sealed correspondence.

I confidently repeat, therefore, the recommendation of my last annual message that the single-rate postage upon drop letters be reduced to one cent wherever the payment of two cents is now required by law. The double rate is only exacted at offices where the carrier system is in operation, and it appears that at those offices the increase in the tax upon local letters defrays the cost not only of its own collection and delivery, but of the collection and delivery of all other mail matter. This is an inequality that ought no longer to exist.

I approve the recommendation of the Postmaster-General that the unit of weight in the rating of first-class matter should be one ounce instead of one-half ounce as it now is. In view of the statistics furnished by the Department it may well be doubted whether the change would result in any loss of revenue; that it would greatly promote the convenience of the public is beyond dispute.

The free-delivery system has been lately applied to five cities, and the total number of offices in which it is now in operation is one hundred and fifty-nine. Experience shows that its adoption, under proper conditions, is equally an accommodation to the public and an advantage to the postal service. It is more than self-sustaining, and for the reasons urged by the Postmaster-General may properly be extended.

In the opinion of that officer it is important to provide means whereby exceptional dispatch in dealing with letters in free-delivery offices may be secured by payment of extraordinary postage. This scheme might be made effective by employment of a special stamp whose cost should be commensurate with the expense of the extra service.

In some of the large cities private express companies have undertaken to outstrip the Government mail-carriers by affording, for the prompt transmission of letters, better facilities than have hitherto been at the command of the Post-Office.

It has always been the policy of the Government to discourage such enterprises, and in no better mode can that policy be maintained than in supplying the public with the most efficient mail service that, with due regard to its own best interests, can be furnished for its accommodation.

The Attorney-General renews the recommendation contained in his report of last year touching the fees of witnesses and jurors.

He favors radical changes in the fee bill, the adoption of a system by which attorneys and marshals of the United States shall be compensated solely by salaries, and the erection by the Government of a penitentiary for the confinement of offenders against its laws.

Of the varied governmental concerns in charge of the Interior Department, the report of its Secretary presents an interesting summary. Among the topics deserving particular attention I refer you to his observations respecting our Indian affairs, the pre-emption and timber-culture acts, the failure of railroad companies to take title to lands granted by the Government, and the operations of the Pension Office, the Patent Office, the Census Bureau, and the Bureau of Education.

Allusion has been made already to the circumstance that, both as between the different Indian tribes and as between the Indians and the whites, the past year has been one of unbroken peace.

In this circumstance the President is glad to find justification for the policy of the Government in its dealing with the Indian question, and confirmation of the views which were fully expressed in his first communication to the Forty-seventh Congress.

The Secretary urges anew the enactment of a statute for the punishment of crimes committed on the Indian reservations, and recommends the passage of the bill now pending in the House of Representatives for the purchase of a tract of 18,000 square miles from the Sioux reservation. Both these measures are worthy of approval.

I concur with him also in advising the repeal of the pre-emption law, the enactment of statutes resolving the present legal complications touching lapsed grants to railroad companies, and the funding of the debt of the several Pacific railroads under such guaranty as shall effectually secure its ultimate payment.

The report of the Utah Commission will be read with interest.

It discloses the results of recent legislation looking to the prevention and punishment of polygamy in that Territory. I still believe
that if that abominable practice can be suppressed by law it can
only be by the most radical legislation consistent with the restraints

I again recommend, therefore, that Congress assume absolute political control of the Territory of Utah, and provide for the appointment of commissioners, with such governmental powers as in its
judgment may justly and wisely be put into their hands.

In the course of this communication reference has more than once
been made to the policy of this Government as regards the extension of our foreign trade. It seems proper to declare the general
principles that should, in my opinion, underlie our national efforts
in this direction.

The main conditions of the problem may be thus stated:

We are a people apt in mechanical pursuits and fertile in invention; we cover a vast extent of territory rich in agricultural products and in nearly all the raw materials necessary for successful
manufacture; we have a system of productive establishments more
than sufficient to supply our own demands; the wages of labor are
nowhere else so great; the scale of living of our artisan classes is
such as tends to secure their personal comfort and the development
of those higher moral and intellectual qualities that go to the making of good citizens. Our system of tax and tariff legislation is
yielding a revenue which is in excess of the present needs of the
Government.

These are the elements from which it is sought to devise a scheme
by which, without unfavorably changing the condition of the work-
ingman, our merchant marine shall be raised from its enfeebled condition and new markets provided for the sale, beyond our borders,
of the manifold fruits of our industrial enterprises.

The problem is complex, and can be solved by no single measure
of innovation or reform.

The countries of the American continent and the adjacent islands
are for the United States the natural marts of supply and demand.
It is from them that we should obtain what we do not produce or do

not produce in sufficiency, and it is to them that the surplus productions of our fields, our mills, and our workshops should flow, under conditions that will equalize or favor them in comparison with foreign competition.

Four paths of policy seem to point to this end.

First, a series of reciprocal commercial treaties with the countries of America which shall foster between us and them an unhampered movement of trade. The conditions of these treaties should be the free admission of such merchandise as this country does not produce, in return for the admission free or under a favored scheme of duties, of our own products—the benefits of such exchange to apply only to goods carried under the flag of the parties to the contract; the removal, on both sides, from the vessels so privileged of all tonnage dues and national imposts so that those vessels may ply unhindered between our ports and those of the other contracting parties, though without infringing on the reserved home coasting trade; the removal or reduction of burdens on the exported products of those countries coming within the benefits of the treaties; and the avoidance of the technical restrictions and penalties by which our intercourse with those countries is at present hampered.

Secondly, the establishment of the consular service of the United States on a salaried footing, thus permitting the relinquishment of consular fees not only as respects vessels under the national flag, but also as respects vessels of the treaty nations carrying goods entitled to the benefits of the treaties.

Thirdly, the enactment of measures to favor the construction and maintenance of a steam carrying marine under the flag of the United States.

Fourthly, the establishment of an uniform currency basis for the countries of America, so that the coined products of our mines may circulate on equal terms throughout the whole system of commonwealths. This would require a monetary union of America, whereby the output of the bullion-producing countries and the circulation of those which yield neither gold nor silver could be adjusted in conformity with the population, wealth, and commercial needs of each. As many of the countries furnish no bullion to the common stock,

21*

the surplus production of our mines and mints might thus be utilized and a step taken toward the general remonetization of silver.

To the accomplishment of these ends, so far as they can be attained by separate treaties, the negotiations already concluded and now in progress have been directed, and the favor which this enlarged policy has thus far received warrants the belief that its operations will ere long embrace all, or nearly all, the countries of this hemisphere.

It is by no means desirable, however, that the policy under consideration should be applied to these countries alone. The healthful enlargement of our trade with Europe, Asia, and Africa should be sought by reducing tariff burdens on such of their wares as neither we nor the other American States are fitted to produce, and thus enabling ourselves to obtain in return a better market for our supplies of food, of raw materials, and of the manufactures in which we excel.

It seems to me that many of the embarrassing elements in the great national conflict between protection and free trade may thus be turned to good account—that the revenue may be reduced so as no longer to overtax the people, that protective duties may be retained without becoming burdensome, that our shipping interests may be judiciously encouraged, the currency fixed on firm bases, and above all such an unity of interests established among the states of the American system as will be of great and ever increasing advantage to them all.

All treaties in the line of this policy which have been negotiated or are in process of negotiation contain a provision deemed to be requisite under the clause of the Constitution limiting to the House of Representatives the authority to originate bills for raising revenue.

On the 29th of February last I transmitted to the Congress the first annual report of the Civil Service Commission, together with communications from the heads of the several Executive Departments of the Government, respecting the practical workings of the law under which the Commission had been acting. The good results therein foreshadowed have been more than realized.

The system has fully answered the expectations of its friends in securing competent and faithful public servants and in protecting the appointing officers of the Government from the pressure of personal importunity and from the labor of examining the claims and pretensions of rival candidates for public employment.

The law has had the unqualified support of the President and of the heads of the several Departments, and the members of the Commission have performed their duties with zeal and fidelity. Their report will shortly be submitted, and will be accompanied by such recommendations for enlarging the scope of the existing statute as shall commend themselves to the Executive and the Commissioners charged with its administration.

In view of the general and persistent demand throughout the commercial community for a national bankrupt law, I hope that the differences of sentiment which have hitherto prevented its enactment may not outlast the present session.

The pestilence which for the past two years has been raging in the countries of the East recently made its appearance in European ports with which we are in constant communication.

The then Secretary of the Treasury, in pursuance of a proclamation of the President, issued certain regulations restricting, and for a time prohibiting, the importation of rags and the admission of baggage of immigrants and of travelers arriving from infected quarters. Lest this course may have been without strict warrant of law, I approve the recommendation of the present Secretary that the Congress take action in the premises, and I also recommend the immediate adoption of such measures as will be likely to ward off the dreaded epidemic, and to mitigate its severity in case it shall unhappily extend to our shores.

The annual report of the Commissioners of the District of Columbia reviews the operations of the several departments of its municipal government. I ask your careful consideration of its suggestions in respect to legislation—especially commending such as relate to a revision of the civil and criminal code, the performance of labor by persons sentenced to imprisonment in the jail, the construction and occupation of wharves along the river front, and the erection of a suitable building for District offices.

Ulysses S. Grant, late General of the Armies of the United States and twice President of this nation, the Congress confer upon him a

Certain of the measures that seem to me necessary and expedient I have now, in obedience to the Constitution, recommended for your adoption.

with renewing the recommendations already made to the Congress, without restating the grounds upon which such recommendations

of Government aid for popular education, the amendment by the Federal Constitution so as to make effective the disapproval by the President of particular items in appropriation bills, the enactment of statutes in regard to the filling of vacancies in the Presidential office, and the determining of vexed questions respecting Presiden-

As the time draws nigh when I am to retire from the public service, I cannot refrain from expressing to the members of the National Legislature with whom I have been brought into personal and official intercourse my sincere appreciation of their unfailing courtesy and of their harmonious co-operation with the Executive in so many measures calculated to promote the best interests of the Nation.

And to my fellow-citizens generally I acknowledge a deep sense of obligation for the support which they have accorded me in my administration of the Executive Department of this Government.

CHESTER A. ARTHUR.

WASHINGTON, *December 1, 1884.*

MESSAGE

TRANSMITTING

A CONVENTION FOR COMMERCIAL RECIPROCITY BETWEEN THE UNITED STATES AND THE DOMINICAN REPUBLIC.

DECEMBER 9, 1884.

MESSAGE.

I transmit herewith, for the consideration of the Senate, with a view to obtaining its advice thereon and consent thereto, a Convention for commercial reciprocity between the United States and the Dominican Republic, which was signed in this Capital on the fourth instant.

This Convention aims to carry out the principles which, as explained in my last annual message to the Congress, should, it is conceived, control all commercial arrangements entered into with our neighbors of the American system with whom trade must be conducted by sea. Santo Domingo is the first of the independent Republics of the Western Hemisphere with which an engagement of this character has been concluded, and the precedent now set will command your fullest attention, as affecting like future negotiations.

CHESTER A. ARTHUR.

Executive Mansion,
Washington, December 9, 1884.

To the Senate and House of Representatives:

MESSAGE

TRANSMITTING

A CONVENTION FOR COMMERCIAL RECIPROCITY BETWEEN THE UNITED STATES AND SPAIN, PROVIDING FOR AN INTIMATE AND FAVORED EXCHANGE OF PRODUCTS WITH THE ISLANDS OF CUBA AND PORTO RICO.

DECEMBER 10, 1884.

MESSAGE.

To the Senate of the United States:

I transmit herewith, for consideration by the Senate with a view to advising and consenting to its ratification, a convention for commercial reciprocity between the United States and Spain, providing for an intimate and favored exchange of products with the islands of Cuba and Porto Rico, which convention was signed at Madrid on the 18th ultimo.

The negotiations for this convention have been in progress since April last, in pursuance of the understanding reached by the two Governments on the 2d of January, 1884, for the improvement of commercial relations between the United States and the Spanish Antilles, by the eighth article of which both Governments engaged "to begin at once negotiations for a complete treaty of commerce and navigation between the United States of America and the said provinces of Cuba and Porto Rico." Although this clause was by common consent omitted from the substitutionary agreement of February 13, 1884 (now in force until replaced by this convention being carried into effect), the obligation to enter upon such a negotiation was deemed to continue. With the best desire manifest on both sides to reach a common accord, the negotiation has been necessarily protracted, owing to the complexity of the details to be incorporated in order that the convention might respond to the national policy of intercourse with the neighboring communities of the American system, which is outlined in my late annual message to the Congress, in the following words:

"The conditions of these treaties should be the free admission of such merchandise as this country does not produce, in return for the admission free, or under a favored scheme of duties, of our own products—the benefits of such exchange to apply only to goods carried under the flag of the parties to the contract; the removal, on both sides, from the vessels so privileged of all tonnage dues and national imposts so that those vessels may ply unhindered between our ports and those of the other contracting parties, though without infringing on the reserved home coasting trade; the removal or reduction of burdens on the exported products of those countries coming within the benefits of the treaties, and the avoidance of the technical restrictions and penalties by which our intercourse with those countries is at present hampered."

A perusal of the convention now submitted will suffice to show how fully it carries out the policy of intercourse thus announced. I commend it to you in the confident expectation that it will receive your sanction.

It does not seem necessary to my present purpose to enter into detailed consideration of the many immediate and prospective advantages which will flow from this convention to our productions and our shipping interests.

CHESTER A. ARTHUR.

EXECUTIVE MANSION,
Washington, December 10, 1884.

MESSAGE.

INTEROCEANIC CANAL ACROSS THE STATE OF NICARAGUA.

DECEMBER 10, 1884.

MESSAGE.

I transmit herewith to the Senate for consideration with a view to ratification, a treaty signed on the first of December with the Republic of Nicaragua, providing for the construction of an interoceanic canal across the territory of that State.

The negotiation of this treaty was entered upon under a conviction that it was imperatively demanded by the present and future political and material interests of the United States.

The establishment of water communication between the Atlantic and Pacific coasts of the Union is a necessity, the accomplishment of which, however, within the territory of the United States is a physical impossibility. While the enterprise of our citizens has responded to the duty of creating means of speedy transit by rail between the two oceans, these great achievements are inadequate to supply a most important requisite of national union and prosperity.

For all maritime purposes, the States upon the Pacific are more distant from those upon the Atlantic than if separated by either ocean alone. Europe and Africa are nearer to New York, and Asia nearer to California, than are these two great States to each other by sea. Weeks of steam voyage, or months under sail, are consumed in the passage around the Horn, with the disadvantage of traversing tempestuous waters, or risking the navigation of the Straits of Magellan.

A nation like ours cannot rest satisfied with such a separation of its mutually dependent members. We possess an ocean border of considerably over ten thousand miles on the Atlantic and Gulf of Mexico, and, including Alaska, of some ten thousand miles on the Pacific. Within a generation the western coast has developed into an empire, with a large and rapidly-growing population, with vast

335

but partially developed resources. At the present rate of increase, the end of the century will see us a commonwealth of perhaps nearly one hundred millions of inhabitants, of which the West should have a considerably larger and richer proportion than now. Forming one nation in interests and aims, the East and the West are more widely disjoined for all purposes of direct and economical intercourse by water, and of national defense against maritime aggression, than are most of the colonies of other powers from their mother country.

attracted attention. Many projects have been formed and surveys have been made of all possible available routes. As a knowledge of the true topical conditions of the Isthmus was gained, insuperable difficulties in one case and another became evident, until by a process of elimination only two routes remained within range of profitable achievement, one by way of Panama, and the other across Nicaragua.

The treaty now laid before you provides for such a waterway, through the friendly territory of Nicaragua.

I invite your special attention to the provisions of the convention itself as best evidencing its scope.

From respect to the independent sovereignty of the Republic, through whose co-operation the project can alone be realized, the stipulations of the treaty look to the fullest recognition and protection of Nicaraguan rights in the premises. The United States have no motive or desire for territorial acquisition or political control beyond their present borders, and none such is contemplated by this treaty. The two Governments unite in framing this scheme as the sole means by which the work, as indispensable to the one as to the other, can be accomplished under such circumstances as to prevent alike the possibility of conflict between them and of interference from without.

The canal is primarily a domestic means of water communication between the Atlantic and Pacific shores of the two countries which unite for its construction, the one contributing the territory and the other furnishing the money therefor. Recognizing the advantages which the world's commerce must derive from the work, appreciating the benefit of enlarged use to the canal itself by contributing to its maintenance and by yielding an interest return on the capital invested therein, and inspired by the belief that any great enterprise which inures to the general benefit of the world is in some sort a trust for the common advancement of mankind, the two Governments have by this treaty provided for its peaceable use by all nations on equal terms, while reserving to the coasting trade of both countries (in which none but the contracting parties are interested) the privilege of favoring tolls.

The treaty provides for the construction of a railway and telegraph line, if deemed advisable, as accessories to the canal, as both may be necessary for the economical construction of the work and probably in its operation when completed.

The terms of the treaty as to the protection of the canal, while scrupulously confirming the sovereignty of Nicaragua, amply secure that State and the work itself from possible contingencies of the future which it may not be within the sole power of Nicaragua to meet.

From a purely commercial point of view the completion of such a waterway opens a most favorable prospect for the future of our country. The nations of the Pacific coast of South America will, by its means, be brought into close connection with our Gulf States. The relation of those American countries to the United States is that of a natural market, from which the want of direct communication has hitherto practically excluded us. By piercing the Isthmus, the heretofore inseparable obstacles of time and sea distance disappear, and our vessels and productions will enter upon the world's competitive field with a decided advantage of which they will avail themselves.

When to this is joined the large coasting trade between the Atlantic and Pacific States which must necessarily spring up, it is evident that this canal affords, even alone, an efficient means of restoring our flag to its former place on the seas.

Such a domestic coasting trade would arise immediately, for even the fishing vessels of both seaboards, which now lie idle in the winter months, could then profitably carry goods between the Eastern and the Western States.

22*

The political effect of the canal will be to knit closer the States

personal intercourse, and it will not only cheapen the cost of transportation but will free individuals from the possibility of unjust dis-

It will bring the European grain markets of demand within easy
distance of our Pacific States, and will give to the manufacturers on
the Atlantic seaboard economical access to the cities of China, thus
breaking down the barrier which separates the principal manufacturing centers of the United States from the markets of the vast
population of Asia, and placing the Eastern States of the Union for
all purposes of trade midway between Europe and Asia.   In point
of time the gain for sailing vessels would be great, amounting from
New York to San Francisco to a saving of seventy-five days, to Hong-
Kong of twenty-seven days, to Shanghai of thirty-four days, and to
Callao of fifty-two days.

Lake Nicaragua is about 90 miles long and 40 miles in greatest
width; the water is fresh and affords abundant depth for vessels of
the deepest draught.   Several islands give facilities for establishing
coaling stations, supply depots, harbors, and places for repairs.   The
advantage of this vast inland harbor is evident.

The lake is 110 feet above tide-water.   Six locks, or five interme
diate levels, are required for the Pacific end of the canal.   On the
Atlantic side but five locks, or four intermediate levels, are proposed.
These locks would, in practice, no more limit the number of vessels
passing through the canal than would the single tide-lock on the
Pacific end, which is necessary to any even or sea-level route.

Seventeen and a half miles of canal lie between the Pacific and
the lake.   The distance across the lake is 56 miles, and a dam at
the mouth of the San Carlos (a tributary of the San Juan), raising
the water level 49 feet, practically extends the lake 63 miles to that
point by a channel from 600 to 1,200 feet wide, with an abundant
depth of water.

From the mouth of the San Carlos (where the canal will leave
the San Juan) to the harbor of Greytown the distance is 36 miles,
which it is hoped may by new surveys be shortened 10 miles.

The total canal excavation would thus be from 43½ to 53½ miles, and the lake and river navigation, amounting to 119 miles by the present survey, would be somewhat increased if the new surveys are successful.

From New York to San Francisco by this route, for sailing vessels, the time is ten days shorter than by the Panama route.

The purely pecuniary prospects of the canal as an investment are subordinate to the great national benefits to accrue from it; but it seems evident that the work, great as its cost may appear, will be a measure of prudent economy and foresight if undertaken simply to afford our own vessels a free waterway, for its far-reaching results will, even within a few years in the life of a nation, amply repay the expenditure by the increase of national prosperity. Further, the canal would unquestionably be immediately remunerative. It offers a shorter sea voyage with more continuously favoring winds between the Atlantic ports of America and Europe and the countries of the east than any other practicable route; and with lower tolls, by reason of its lesser cost, the Nicaragua route must be the interoceanic highway for the bulk of the world's trade between the Atlantic and the Pacific.

So strong is this consideration that it offers an abundant guarantee for the investment to be made, as well as for the speedy payment of the loan of four millions which the treaty stipulates shall be made to Nicaragua for the construction of internal improvements to serve as aids to the business of the canal.

I might suggest many other considerations in detail, but it seems unnecessary to do so. Enough has been said to more than justify the practical utility of the measure. I therefore commit it to the Congress in the confident expectation that it will receive approval, and that by appropriate legislation means may be provided for inaugurating the work without delay after the treaty shall have been ratified.

In conclusion, I urge the justice of recognizing the aid which has recently been rendered in this matter by some of our citizens. The efforts of certain gentlemen connected with the American company which received the concession from Nicaragua (now terminated and replaced by this international compact) accomplished much of the preliminary labors leading to the conclusion of the treaty.

You may have occasion to examine the matter of their services, when such further information as you may desire will be furnished you.

I may add that the canal can be constructed by the able Engineer Corps of our Army, under their thorough system, cheaper and better than any work of such magnitude can in any other way be built.

CHESTER A. ARTHUR.

EXECUTIVE MANSION,
　　　Washington, December 10, 1884.

ADDRESS.

THE WORLD'S INDUSTRIAL AND COTTON CENTENNIAL EXPOSITION.

DECEMBER 16, 1884.

341

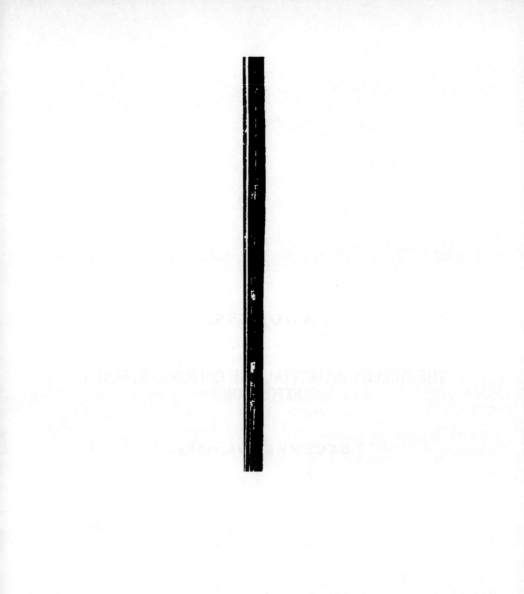

ADDRESS.

In the name of the people of the Republic, I congratulate the citizens of the Southwest in their advancing prosperity as manifested by the great International Exposition now about to open.

The interest of the nation in that section of our commonwealth has found expression in many ways and notably in appropriations for the improvement of the Mississippi and in the national loan to promote the present Exposition.

Situated as it is, at the gateway of the trade between the United States and Central and South America, it will attract the attention of the people of the neighboring nations of the American system and they will learn the importance of availing themselves of our products as we will of theirs, and thus, not only good feeling but a profitable intercourse between the United States, the States of Central and South America, will be promoted.

The people also of our own country, thus brought closer together, will find, in this Exposition of competitive industries, motives for strengthening the bonds of brotherhood.

Railroads, telegraph lines, and submarine cables have drawn much nearer the nations of the earth, and an assembly like this of the representatives of different nations is promotive of good-will and peace, while it advances the material welfare of all. The United States extend, to those from foreign countries who visit us on this occasion, a cordial welcome.

And now, at the Executive Mansion in Washington, in the presence of the assembled representatives of the friendly nations of the world, of the President of the Senate, of the Speaker of the House of Representatives, the Chief Justice and Associate Justices of the Supreme Court, of a Committee from each House of Congress and of the Members of my Cabinet, I again, and in their name, congrat-

343

ulate the promoters of the Exposition upon the auspicious inauguration of an enterprise which promises such far-reaching results.

With my best wishes for the fulfillment of all its great purposes,
I now declare that the World's Industrial and Cotton Centennial
Exposition is open.

EXECUTIVE MANSION,
Washington, December 16, 1884.

MESSAGE

CONCERNING THE

MILITARY AND CIVIL TESTIMONIALS TO GENERAL GRANT.

FEBRUARY 3, 1885.

MESSAGE.

I take especial pleasure in laying before Congress the generous offer made by Mrs. Grant to give to the Government, in perpetual trust, the swords and military and civil testimonials lately belonging to General Grant. A copy of the deed of trust, and of a letter addressed to me by Mr. William H. Vanderbilt, which I transmit herewith, will explain the nature and motives of this offer.

Appreciation of General Grant's achievements and recognition of his just fame have in part taken the shape of numerous mementos and gifts, which, while dear to him, possess for the nation an exceptional interest. These relics, of great historical value, have passed into the hands of another whose considerate action has restored the collection to Mrs. Grant as a life trust, on the condition that at the death of General Grant, or sooner at Mrs. Grant's option, it should become the property of the Government, as set forth in the accompanying papers. In the exercise of the option thus given her, Mrs. Grant elects that the trust shall forthwith determine, and asks that the Government designate a suitable place of deposit and a responsible custodian for the collection.

The nature of this gift and the value of the relics which the generosity of a private citizen, joined to the high sense of public regard which animates Mrs. Grant, have thus placed at the disposal of the Government, demand full and signal recognition, on behalf of the nation, at the hands of its representatives. I therefore ask Congress to take suitable action to accept the trust and to provide for its secure custody, at the same time recording the appreciative gratitude of the people of the United States to the donors.

In this connection, I may pertinently advert to the pending legislation of the Senate and House of Representatives, looking to a national recognition of General Grant's eminent services by providing the means for his restoration to the Army on the retired list. That Congress, by taking such action, will give expression to the almost universal desire of the people of this nation, is evident, and I earnestly urge the passage of an act similar to Senate bill No. 2530, which, while not interfering with the Constitutional prerogative of appointment, will enable the President in his discretion to nominate General Grant as General upon the retired list.

CHESTER A. ARTHUR.

EXECUTIVE MANSION,
February 3, 1885.

MESSAGE

TRANSMITTING

THE SECOND ANNUAL REPORT OF THE UNITED STATES CIVIL SERVICE COMMISSION.

FEBRUARY 11, 1885.

MESSAGE

To the Senate and House of Representatives:

In compliance with the act of Congress approved January 16, 1883, entitled "An act to regulate and improve the civil service of the United States," the Civil Service Commission has made to the President its second annual report.

That report is herewith transmitted.

The Commission is in the second year of its existence. The President congratulates the country upon the success of its labors, commends the subject to the favorable consideration of Congress, and asks for an appropriation to continue the work.

CHESTER A. ARTHUR.

Executive Mansion,
Washington, February 11, 1885.

Lightning Source UK Ltd.
Milton Keynes UK
UKHW021206180219
337529UK00010B/528/P